THE ESSENTIAL GUIDE TO FINANCIAL INDEPENDENCE

PURPOSE, BALANCE, AND FREEDOM

The Essential Guide to Financial Independence blends corporate-level principles with personal finance, distilling decades of market experience into a practical, actionable guide for individuals seeking financial independence – demonstrating how the frameworks used by the world's largest firms can be adapted to personal financial planning and work for anyone with disciplined execution.

The book empowers individuals to take control of their financial future through thoughtful planning, smart saving, and disciplined investing. It provides tools to understand income needs, build a sustainable finance portfolio, avoid common investing mistakes, and integrate financial decisions with broader life goals – ultimately helping readers or their clients create a balanced, purposeful life where money supports, rather than dictates, their choices. It enables you to:

- Construct a personalised financial plan tailored to your life goals.
- Determine how much you need to save for a secure retirement.
- Avoid the pitfalls of over-saving and missing out on meaningful life experiences.
- Above all, align your purpose in life with achieving financial independence and what you will do with it.

Independent Financial Advisors will find in-depth analysis, holistic frameworks, and case studies that can enhance their professional practice and broaden their toolkit for advising clients. It also bridges the gap between professional finance and personal money management and offers actionable insights grounded in real-world financial practice for individual investors.

László Bencsics is a seasoned Treasury professional with a 25+ year career spanning market risk management, dealing, and consulting, advising top firms across both banking and corporate sectors.

"In a marketplace crowded with 'get rich quick' schemes, László delivers a professional-grade masterclass in financial independence. As a 30-year veteran of corporate finance, I have seen how the most successful organizations manage risk and capital; László has brilliantly translated these high-level disciplines for the individual reader.

I recognize the power of his framework: it is a rare combination of mathematical precision and holistic wisdom. This book provides the tools to stop sleepwalking through a career and start intentionally building a life of purpose."

Richard Garry, *Director of Group Treasury, Insurance and Pensions*

"So happy to see László's knowledge and experience being channelled into something so practical. I love the concept behind *The Essential Guide to Financial Independence* – honestly, who wouldn't benefit from a clear, structured guide like this? It's a book a lot of people need…"

Julia Tyutrina, *C Suite Finance and Business Transformation Consultant, Finance Coach for Start-up CEOs, Speaker*

"I'm incredibly proud to see this book out in the world. It stands out for its clear, practical approach to personal finance, offering guidance that feels accessible, supportive, and free of judgment. Rather than overwhelming readers with jargon, it meets them where they are and helps them take meaningful, manageable steps forward.

More than just advice, this book builds confidence. It feels like having a trusted friend by your side, guiding you toward a healthier relationship with money. For anyone feeling uncertain or stuck, it provides the clarity and encouragement needed to turn good intentions into real progress."

Mahesh Ramaswamy, *Senior Director*

"Wow, I think most people would be interested! The life hack I've been looking for…"

Paul Nemes, *Chief Operating Officer*

THE ESSENTIAL GUIDE TO FINANCIAL INDEPENDENCE

PURPOSE, BALANCE, AND FREEDOM

László Bencsics

Routledge
Taylor & Francis Group
LONDON AND NEW YORK

Designed cover image: Getty Images Credit: artisteer
Illustrations: Dóra Grausz

First published 2027
by Routledge
4 Park Square, Milton Park, Abingdon, Oxon OX14 4RN

and by Routledge
605 Third Avenue, New York, NY 10158

Routledge is an imprint of the Taylor & Francis Group, an informa business

British Library Cataloguing-in-Publication Data
A catalogue record for this book is available from the British Library

ISBN: 978-1-041-34365-3 (hbk)
ISBN: 978-1-041-30737-2 (pbk)
ISBN: 978-1-003-79244-4 (ebk)

DOI: 10.4324/9781003792444

Typeset in Bembo
by Taylor & Francis Books

For my family

CONTENTS

ABOUT THE AUTHOR

As one of my colleagues said, "What I really want to know from an author's bio is why should I listen to you?" You're probably wondering the same thing. So, here's what I think you'd want to know before deciding whether to dive into this book.

I've been a Treasury professional for 27 years and counting. I have always sought to be an all-round one. As a result, my career has been split, almost evenly, between working in banking, multinational corporations, and project or consulting roles (covering both) – more than five years of which were spent in the Treasury Advisory practice of a Big 4 firm.

Of the experiences I draw on explicitly in the book, the best part of ten years was in market risk management-related roles and a number not far off that in "front-office" market-facing and dealing roles. Consulting and project management gave me a mindset where you start with the desired goal – or "to be" – and work backwards to construct a plan to get there.

I've had a keen interest in financial markets since I was about 16, which made my choice of career almost inevitable. Over the past three decades, I've gained direct experience as an investor, navigating the dot-com crash, the financial crisis of 2008, and the long bull market that followed. As chance would have it, I witnessed the dot-com crash while working in a bank's market risk management department and the financial crisis from a bank's dealing desk – each giving me a unique perspective.

I also have hands-on experience with buy-to-let investments and a solid understanding of the principles behind the FIRE (Financial Independence, Retire Early) movement. Thanks to my professional background, I believe I weigh up FIRE concepts differently than some others. While I find much of the logic valuable – and some of it has even made its way into this book – I've also taken an objective approach to highlight potential pitfalls.

Over the years, I've had many conversations with non-expert friends, which have given me insight into the questions people want a professional's perspective on.

I have tried to blend all of the above – theory, a little bit of philosophy, and practical implementation techniques – into a one-stop shop that I hope will provide value to fellow professionals and non-experts alike. I've written this book to be accessible to everyone, and I hope you'll find it both valuable and enjoyable.

László

1

INTRODUCTION

WHAT IS FINANCIAL INDEPENDENCE?

How much do you value your personal freedom? The freedom to spend your time how you would like to spend it? Financial independence means having enough savings and investments to sustain your desired lifestyle without needing to work. In other words, having the funds to do what you would like, without worrying about whether you have the time or the money to afford to do so.

Financial independence can mean different things to different people. At its heart it is a quality-of-life question. One of living life on your own terms whilst providing you with financial peace of mind. Imagine not having to worry about job security or how to meet unexpected expenses. Being financially independent means you can make decisions based on what you want to do, or on other values, rather than financial necessity. Without the pressure, you can choose a career that you love, improve your work–life balance, and devote more time to family or a hobby. You can move to working fewer hours, part-time, or taking more time off.

Your investment pot can provide you an income that hasn't been earned through an exchange of your time for money (unlike a salary). A sort of bonus and one that could provide you with an income that you wouldn't otherwise have.

You also have the freedom to pursue passion projects, volunteer, or start a business without having to worry so much about the financial viability. You can invest in personal development such as learning new skills. You could write a book. You could also choose to leave a legacy.

DOI: 10.4324/9781003792444-1

THINKING BEYOND SALARIES AND PENSIONS

While you are working, the main source of financial stability, for most people, will be a salary. We exchange our time for money. Through this exchange, the regular income we receive covers everything from living costs and expenses to lifestyle. But our time is limited (and our labour is also limited). One day we won't be able to work and make this exchange anymore. So, you will need to put aside some of the output of your labour into financial assets. These can support you when your labour no longer can.

Traditionally, financial independence and retirement were most likely to have meant the same thing. Once upon a time, planning for life after work was easy. You could get a predictable fixed income based on salary and years of service, if you were prepared to work to the standard retirement age.

> In the past, most workers were members of Defined Benefit (DB) pensions ... pensioners do not need to worry about how to invest the amount saved in their pension. The company or employer offering the DB pension (sponsor) assumes the risks.[1]

Pension income simply replaced salaried income once you were old enough to qualify. Final Salary or Defined Benefit (DB) pension schemes were once common. You would pay into one, and after retirement you received a predictable income guaranteed for life. Complemented by the state pension, this system meant retirees could be financially secure without a need to become particularly involved in the subtleties of financial planning.

These worked well for employees. However, with people living longer, this meant that pension schemes needed to sustain pay-outs for longer as well. Regulations also became stricter and required employers to fully fund pension liabilities, increasing the financial burden further. Unfortunately, for individuals that world is now largely gone. In the UK, the burden of retirement planning has shifted, and shifted onto you. This is the case whether you like it or not.

Pension schemes began to transition towards so-called Defined Contribution (DC) schemes. Although employers and employees continue to contribute to the employee's pot, the ultimate outcome shifted to depend on the level of contributions made, how the contributions are invested (asset allocation and fund selection), time horizon, and the investment performance, among other factors.

Defined Contribution schemes, though, throw up a lot of opportunity but they also mean that you must become proactive in managing your pot. You must determine how much you might need, how much to save to get there, how to invest it, how long you might need your portfolio to last. You must also learn about tax efficiency and sustainable withdrawal rates, and have the discipline to keep going each month for years. That is a big ask for the average person.

The good news is that there are useful tools and rules of thumb available to help you get started. This book seeks to help you set the guiderails you need. By their nature, rules of thumb are designed for broad use and to apply across a wide range of scenarios. But once you know something about these tools and how they work, you can apply them to suit your own timeline and personal ambitions about the lifestyle you would like to lead.

In other words, although you are now forced to plan and take ownership of your own financial future, the freedoms available to you after you do are now greater than ever. Investing has grown more "democratised," but there is now more risk in not planning than ever before.

BEING FINANCIALLY INDEPENDENT AND RICH

It is easy to mix the terms financially independent with being rich. For many people the two terms seem to be interchangeable. In some cases, entirely justifiably as someone can be both rich and financially independent. But there are other cases where the two do not overlap at all. Sometimes, they represent fundamentally different approaches to wealth and life satisfaction. Achieving financial independence with a more modest standard of living is certainly achievable in a faster timeframe than with a rich, lavish lifestyle.

For some people, being financially independent may mean a focus on freedom and sustainable living, focusing on the security aspects of achieving financial independence. They will have achieved it with a lot of discipline, and long-term planning. The value of someone's time without depending on a salary may be highlighted as the real wealth in such cases, rather than overt displays of financial wealth, and the ability to afford the luxurious.

As Morgan Housel puts it in his book *The Art of Spending Money*, "Rich … means not being hurried, spending time with my family, control over my schedule, and intellectual independence … Independence. That's true rich."[2]

Some people who are in the possession of accumulated objective wealth, may be entrepreneurs, have been lucky enough to receive a large inheritance, or been the beneficiaries of generational wealth. Some may have had high-powered careers with accompanying benefits and bonuses. For people in any of these categories, showcasing social status may take on an increased importance.

At their heart, the two scenarios can represent entirely different attitudes not just to lifestyle but to money itself.

THE HIDDEN COST OF STATUS: HOW EGO IMPACTS WEALTH BUILDING

For most people, there is a direct link between financial trajectory and an individual's relationship with status. "Not needing to impress other people … is an asset on your personal balance sheet that can be more valuable than anything else."[3]

"Ego"-driven spending, an attachment to material possessions, and status-seeking behaviours all come with a price tag in terms of long-term wealth accumulation. "Someone driving a $100,000 car might be wealthy. But the only data point you have about their wealth is that they have $100,000 less than they did before they bought the car (or $100,000 more debt) … [but] we tend to judge wealth by what we see."[4]

Tying self-worth to material possessions introduces a double financial burden. Firstly, there is the direct impact on spending. Not only does expenditure increase but saving capacity inversely declines. By trying to look rich, many individuals are essentially acquiring liabilities. A dangerous pattern can emerge where consumption raises proportionally with income and perpetuates going forward. Not only can this represent a significant obstacle to building genuine wealth, but it elevates the financial threshold required to maintain this lifestyle. At the same time, it acts to prevent the ability to accumulate the capital necessary to achieve financial independence.

For some, attaching a marker of success onto material possessions can actively lure individuals towards diminished financial security.

REDEFINING WEALTH

Ironically, the wealthiest individuals can be those who feel the least compulsion to use visible consumption to demonstrate their financial position. True wealth can bring with it a quiet confidence as well as a shift away from conspicuous consumption. Real wealth does not require external validation. It does not need to prove itself. It means having enough and being content with this. It manifests in a sense of sufficiency and contentment, not comparative status. You no longer need to prove yourself to others. If your self-worth now comes from within, you free yourself to focus on what really matters to you. Then you can call yourself truly wealthy.

Financial maturity can bring with it a psychological reorientation then with a decoupling of self-worth from material displays and toward meaningful financial objectives. This isn't about extreme frugality or deprivation – it's about intentional spending aligned with personal values.

The key distinction is mindful consumption versus status-driven spending. Understanding whether particular expenditures truly enhance well-being, or merely signal status, accelerates wealth accumulation, without sacrificing quality of life. This balanced approach, neither wasteful status spending, nor extreme deprivation, creates sustainable wealth, while supporting a fulfilling lifestyle redirecting resources toward increasing savings and investing in appreciating assets. This has twofold benefits both in increased savings but also in reduced lifestyle inflation. In this sense, the resulting financial discipline can be the gateway to sustainable wealth creation. Therefore, understanding the psychological dimensions of expenditure can be just as important as investment strategy.

THIS BOOK

Welcome to a different kind of personal finance book. One that applies the principles used by banks and corporate professionals to personal finance, grounded in real-world financial markets and corporate governance. The book is structured thematically in the following way: foundational concepts (Chapters 1–2), practical mechanics (Chapters 3–7), investment strategy (Chapters 8–14), psychological resilience (Chapters 15–17), and implementation (Chapters 18–22)

Many books focusing on FIRE (Financial Independence, Retire Early) emphasise aggressive saving and investing so practitioners can "FIRE" – that is, achieving financial independence and retiring decades before normal retirement age. While FIRE approaches usefully highlight the relationship between income, expenses, savings rate, and investments, they often swing to the opposite extreme of status-seeking, prescribing austerity measures that can be equally unsustainable for many people.

This book charts a middle path. Drawing on over 25 years as a financial professional in both financial institutions and recognisable multinational corporations (plus 30+ years as a private investor myself), it brings concepts from professional treasury to the personal sphere. The principles guiding multinational corporations in managing billions can be equally powerful when applied to your household finances.

Just as a corporate treasurer balances liquidity needs, investment returns, and risk management to support company strategy, you can structure your personal finances to support your life goals. Treasury isn't simply about managing cash; it's about strategically aligning a financial portfolio with long-term objectives, an approach that can revolutionise your personal finances.

Time is a key ingredient in this financial recipe. With more of it, time does much of the work. Scrimping and saving everything possible rarely leads to life satisfaction and is often unnecessary. That's not how real wealth is created. While the relationship between spending and accumulating the required funds is important (and we'll examine this dynamic), you won't find chapters filled with spending hacks.

Instead, this book aims to develop your understanding of available financial tools, empowering you to make informed decisions that create the best possible life: one where financial worry is absent and what truly matters to you takes centre stage.

The book intentionally drops the "R" and "E" (Retire Early) from the title, while emphasising "F" and "I" (Financial Independence). This doesn't mean you can't use these techniques to FIRE – you absolutely can – but there's no need to rush.

This book serves both the average person interested in their financial future and financial practitioners. For everyday readers, it offers clear, practical guidance and actionable strategies toward long-term financial security and independence. The content demystifies complex financial concepts, making them accessible and relevant to daily life.

Simultaneously, Financial Planners and Independent Financial Advisors will find in-depth analysis, holistic frameworks, and case studies to enhance their professional practice and broaden their client advisory toolkit (with a guide that helps individuals establish initial financial targets and ballpark figures as they begin their financial journey, normally well before they formally engage advisory services). This balanced approach ensures equal value for those seeking personal empowerment and professionals pursuing ongoing development.

SOME CONCLUDING THOUGHTS

Your own life is as unique as your financial situation, goals, and personal circumstances –including health, family obligations, lifestyle preferences, and needs. Sadly, there isn't simply a one-size-fits-all approach. The use of any tools that rely on generic formulas and rules of thumb will have some flaws, but even with their imperfections, they can still be incredibly valuable as a starting point, to help you set up your initial targets, and as generic guideposts to steer your planning in a direction that can help you get to the right "landing area." Far better, to have a plan that you can revisit and tweak as your circumstances change than to leave this to your future self to deal with later, with no real guiderails until then.

Applying points of reference can open a range of life possibilities well beyond simply planning for a standard retirement. If you understand how, for example, you can plan to retire years early, or set your pot to do the work, so that it does much of the hard work, and in the meantime, you can make lifestyle choices free from financial worry.

For some people, financial independence can mean early retirement, for others simply retirement at the usual age, safe in the knowledge that they have a considered plan, and the plans they have are well-funded – or that they can leave a substantial legacy.

NOTES

1. Lustig, Yoram *Saving and Investing for Retirement. The Definitive Handbook to Securing Your Financial Future* (Financial Times Guides, Pearson 2016), page 1.
2. Housel, Morgan *The Art of Spending Money – Simple Choices for a Richer Life* (Harriman House, 2025), page 135.
3. Housel, Morgan *The Art of Spending Money – Simple Choices for a Richer Life* (Harriman House, 2025), page 61.
4. Housel, Morgan *The Psychology of Money* (Harriman House, 2020), page 97.

REFERENCES

Housel, Morgan *The Art of Spending Money – Simple Choices for a Richer Life* (Harriman House, 2025).

Housel, Morgan *The Psychology of Money* (Harriman House, 2020).

Lustig, Yoram *Saving and Investing for Retirement. The Definitive Handbook to Securing Your Financial Future* (Financial Times Guides, Pearson, 2016).

2

YOUR MONEY OR YOUR LIFE

BUYING BACK YOUR TIME

"Your money or your life" is a question that for most of us is not quite as binary as the images of a Western style hold-up conjure. However, the trade-off between them is one we sign up to in practice throughout our lives.

Juggling time, health, and wealth for many people is a balancing act of unequal sides.[1] We may wish to be able to maximise each of these resources at our disposal, but usually we end up minimising one at the expense of maximising the other two. How this plays out changes as we age.

When we go out to work, we sell our time and employ our health to obtain money in the form of a salary. Then throughout our careers we put aside some of this money to pay for a time when we have worked enough and can exchange this money to buy time (and frequently we try to buy health as well).

This translates to a typical life lived starting with initial scarcity of wealth at the outset, time sacrificed to remediate this, and a lack of health by the time we have enough financial resources to be able to "buy back" our time.

THE WEALTH SCARCITY OF YOUTH

Through the lens of youth, time can seem limitless. We have such a vast abundance of time, in fact (and if we are lucky health and high energy levels, too), that with financial resources being the limiting factor, trading time and energy to earn a salary seems a logical strategy.

DOI: 10.4324/9781003792444-2

So, many people end up sleepwalking into a traditional career and retirement plan by default. It is easy not to focus on financial planning when time can seem so unlimited, particularly because a lot of upfront effort will have gone into setting out on a career path to begin with (such as taking a degree and getting relevant work experience). It can be very tempting to reap an immediate dividend for this through lifestyle inflation the second we finally start earning a salary. Many will also be starting careers with a mountain of student debt and no shortage of claims on their pay cheque.

THE TIME SCARCITY OF MIDDLE AGE

By middle age, individuals may frequently be reaching their earning peak, perhaps as early as age 47 according to a *Daily Telegraph* article.[2] Demands on that income may also be high.

Time management can become much more of a challenge. Family responsibilities interweave with career ambitions and personal goals. It is frequently only once an individual is established on the property ladder – and has set their family on a given life trajectory – that attention may eventually shift to retirement planning.

Many individuals will find themselves firmly trapped in the "rat race" at this point, as lifestyle inflation has kept pace with increased earnings through their career to date. It is also very easy to assume that peak earnings will continue indefinitely. Certainly, health may remain robust and may even support intensive work periods, but there is an emerging cost of neglecting health in the pursuit of wealth accumulation.

THE HEALTH SCARCITY OF LATER LIFE

By the time, later in life, we become eligible for state pension and other benefits, time will be at a premium and perhaps the most precious commodity that we possess. Yet after decades focusing on wealth accumulation, it can be very difficult to break with an accumulation mindset and shift to one of decumulation, where we can finally enjoy the fruits of our labour. Instead, many opt for continuing to optimize wealth accumulation. This is unfortunate, as the healthy years of retirement may be limited and sequentially likely to be front-loaded. Maintaining health should likely be at the centre of our focus (and in fact may even require financial resources to support it).

THE TRADITIONAL WAY TO MANAGE OUR PERSONAL RESOURCES

Another way of looking at this traditional path to retirement and financial independence is:

Youth = health and time > wealth
Middle age = health and wealth > time
Old age = wealth and [free] time > health.

The traditional approach of 40 years of hard work then retiring maximises the opportunities for wealth accumulation but can come with significant costs to time and health. Retirement planning along these lines assumes selling 40 years of time and health for wealth and then reversing that trade. However, that can lead to a very unbalanced outcome. "Most folk die with more than 60 per cent of peak lifetime assets."[3]

If we view wealth as a bank of time, unless the intention is to deliberately leave an inheritance or legacy, this translates to a lot of unnecessarily unlived experiences.

Others never move beyond living from one payday to the next and face a poor retirement where they are unable to maintain the lifestyle that they have become accustomed to. In fact, "80% of people work their entire lives while saving very little and they don't invest unless forced to by their employer in the form of pension contributions."[4]

As Robert Kiyosaki neatly summarises in his book *Rich Dad, Poor Dad*, "without financial training, we all too often use the standard formulas to get through life: work hard, save, borrow, and pay excessive taxes."[5]

TIME: THE ULTIMATE RESOURCE

Oliver Burkeman begins his book *Four Thousand Weeks: Time Management for Mortals* with the following observation:

> the real problem isn't our limited time. The real problem ... is that we've unwittingly inherited, and feel pressured to live by, a troublesome set of ideas about how to use our limited time, all of which are pretty much guaranteed to make things worse.[6]

We are inundated with information about how to be ever increasingly productive and cram more and more into our days to be as efficient as possible. The challenges of daily time management overshadow the big picture and are rarely equated with the larger question of how best to use our 4,000 or so weeks.

If we do the calculation, 4,000 weeks translates to about 77 years. However, no one knows exactly how much time they get. (In the UK, the Office for National Statistics publishes a calculator that, based on averages, can give you some guidance as to life expectancy).[7] The point is that our time is limited. If we remain cognisant of that fact maybe we will make different decisions and prioritise different things. *If you knew you might only read another 25 books, which would you choose?*

Time is finite and becomes progressively more valuable the scarcer it becomes.

HEALTH: THE FOUNDATION OF EVERYTHING

A popular urban legend has it that the lifespan of partners at the Big 4 professional services firms is 67 years. The argument goes that the demands of the job, stress, and the hard work required to get there eventually take their toll. If there is any merit in this, it is likely accurate for other firms and high-pressure professions.

It is undeniable that health is different from our other two resources. It is easy to take it for granted while we have it, yet difficult, if not outright impossible, to fully regain it once it is significantly compromised. Without it, time is a burden and wealth only has utility in that it can help us manage the decline of health perhaps a little better.

Whereas time declines gradually but steadily, and the inverse can be true for wealth, health may seem much more stable but with occasional sharp drops.

The health dimension, therefore, is an indispensable part of our financial planning journey. The pursuit of wealth can lead to poor work–life balance, stress, and perhaps even delayed medical care – so we must make active plans to preserve it. Wealth can buy better healthcare, but if we neglect health itself while we accumulate wealth, we can ultimately be landed with higher medical costs. This not only has a direct impact on how much we can have left in our investments but ultimately also on our ability to enjoy the freedom that that wealth can buy.

WEALTH: STORED TIME AND ENERGY

Walking along the Downs Link footpath on a beautiful June day, I stumbled across some graffiti on what I took to be the rump of a half-gone old brick bridge: "Money = Slavery." My immediate thought was no it isn't; rather, "Money = Freedom."

Money is sometimes perceived as an ultimate goal in life. It is better understood, though, as an enabler. Viewing money in such a way is helpful to shift the focus away from having it for its own sake, and an accumulation mindset, to one of utility for the achievement of broader aspirations and life objectives.

Wealth can be viewed as a bank of time – the accumulated store of past labour and energy that can be converted back into time, options, and freedom. Indeed, unlike our other two resources, wealth can continue growing, even while we sleep and even beyond our lifespans.

Time, though, because it is finite, becomes progressively more valuable the scarcer it becomes. The purpose of financial independence, really, is to own more of your time rather than being required to exchange it for money. Morgan Housel is correct when he surmises "that whole idea – trading money for time … is probably the most overlooked aspect of spending money."[8]

WORK–LIFE OPTIMISATION

Understanding the interplay between our resources of time, health, and wealth can mean we can look beyond the traditional approach, rebalance, and think strategically about financial independence at different life stages. This goes beyond the question of simple work–life balance and becomes one of optimisation across your entire lifespan.

In practice, for some people, financial independence can become a question of career compression, and the trade-offs required to minimise the timeline required to reach it. But financial independence can also simply mean being intentional about the life you choose to live and how you choose to balance the relationship between time, health, and wealth – and when.

There isn't really a right answer to this, and your response to these fundamental questions is likely to be as individual as your life and personal circumstances are. Regardless, this book aims to be your guide to help you understand the trade-offs involved in practice, financially, to allow you to make informed decisions. Then it will give you the tools to help you design a financial plan that aligns with your aims – allowing you to be deliberate and not just captured by the default setting of the traditional approach.

For now, there are some underlying questions to consider. Keep in mind that what can seem like small choices can greatly compound over decades.

1 LIFESTYLE DESIGN

Put simply, the simpler the lifestyle you need to fund, the lower the required wealth level needed to fund it. However, "living below your means" is not just about saving money. Rather than living an unnecessarily frugal life, this can translate into discovering what truly matters to you and designing a lifestyle that is sustainable before and after financial independence.

2 TIMELINE

How early do you want to be financially free? Higher savings rates can translate to earlier financial freedom, but so too can accepting lower peak wealth in exchange for more years of freedom.

3 CAREER CHOICE

Do you want to maximise income or pursue a career that is more of a passion and sustainable over the long haul, rather than simply being financially rewarding?

Of course, to have a career that aligns with your sense of purpose and is financially rewarding is a great sweet spot to be in. For others, deciding to maximise income to be able to buy time earlier is a trade they are willing to make. Others, still, may choose a career path they view as sustainable even if it reduces peak wealth but comes with the benefit of non-financial gains such as getting back time and health while still retaining the ability to make steady and consistent progress towards financial independence.

It is worth weighing up this decision carefully, as it essentially concerns your life's work.

As Scott Galloway points out in his book *The Algebra of Wealth: A Simple Formula for Success*:

> believing you have to be passionate about something before embarking on the uphill journey to mastery will lead you to careers where the supply of eager workers far exceeds demand ... only 2% of professional actors make a living from their craft.[9]

He continues: "following your passion isn't just bad for your career, it's bad for your passion. Work is hard, and it comes with setbacks, injustice and disappointment."[10]

This doesn't mean that you shouldn't follow your passion. The question is more about when. It might be a better fit, for example, after you have achieved financial independence, or taken care of your financial future first.

NON-NEGOTIABLES

Whatever your take on how balance looks like in your life, a couple of things could be viewed as non-negotiables. By that I mean things that you shouldn't view as part of any exchange.

1 INVESTMENT IN HEALTH

Quite simply, any wealth or time you put into furthering your health should be viewed as an investment in your ability to enjoy the freedom afforded by the wealth that you are accumulating. Any money that you spend on eating healthily, exercising – even stress reduction – shouldn't, therefore, be viewed as just another expense.

2 INVESTMENT IN RELATIONSHIP MAINTENANCE

Similarly, relationships and social connections are crucial for mental health and life satisfaction when we pull back from work and have more time on our hands. It is important not to neglect these even when we may feel more time-constrained during the wealth accumulation phase of life.

REVISITING THE SEASONS OF LIFE

As the balance between time, health, and wealth changes throughout our lives, each season brings with it its own advantages and constraints. Rather than trying to fight against these realities, an effective financial strategy can focus on how to utilise what is already abundant during each season. By maintaining a long-term perspective on work–life optimisation, we can make decisions that are appropriate for the present while deliberately laying the foundations for the stages that follow.

1 YOUTH: TIME RICH, HEALTH RICH, WEALTH POOR

What is often lacking in wealth during youth is more than offset by an abundance of time and health.

Time allows for the acquisition of skills, education, and experience – in other words, investment in personal development. Decisions made here can echo for decades but don't have to. Fewer fixed obligations can translate into a higher appetite for risk with plenty of recovery time available for any setbacks. All-in-all, this can be a great time for experimentation, even career pivots.

- Working on maximizing future earning potential can make more sense than an early focus on aggressive saving from a limited income.
- That said, it is easy to underestimate the power of starting early. Even modest, regular saving can have an outsized impact over long enough time horizons, and habit formation can serve you well in the decades to come.
- It is a good time for geographic arbitrage while responsibilities are minimal.

- Prioritization of education, skill development, and experiences can all increase long-term earning power.

2 MID-CAREER: TIME POOR, HEALTH RICH, WEALTH RICH

This can be the golden period for wealth accumulation. You may be at your peak earning power at the same time your financial obligations begin falling away. Children may become independent, and you may even have either paid off (or at least taken a serious dent out of) your mortgage.

Lifestyle inflation can be very damaging at this point. After years of financial juggling, it's tempting to "live for now" just when aggressive saving could dramatically accelerate your financial independence timeline. Key strategic considerations during this season of life can include the following:

- This may be the final chance to run a high savings rate. Your earning potential at this point is likely at the high-water mark as could be your career and professional network.
- At the same time your health may still support a more intense schedule (if needed). However, do weigh up and monitor health and relationship costs if considering this.
- Give serious consideration to the transition to financial independence. This can involve time with a financial advisor, considering how you want to spend time in retirement, and evaluating whether lifestyle inflation is (really) worth delaying financial independence for.

3 LATER LIFE: TIME AND HEALTH DECLINING, WEALTH RICH

In later life, time and health often become your most limited resources, even as wealth may be abundant. The ONS publishes data on "Healthy" Life Expectancy (HLE) for the UK.[11] In contrast to actual life expectancy, Healthy Life Expectancy represents how long individuals can expect to live (on average) before developing a major health issue and losing their health.

According to this data, at birth, Healthy Life Expectancy for males ranges from 61.1 years for Wales to 62.4 years in England. The range for females is from 60.3 to 62.7 years, respectively. The trend for Healthy Life Expectancy is that it's falling. The figures for 2020–2022 (although COVID-19 no doubt had an impact) showed that in comparison to 2011–2013, Healthy Life Expectancy decreased by an average of 9.3 and 14.0 months, respectively (in England).

(Disability-free life expectancy is 65.) Crucially, both are below the state retirement age, which is a strong reason why bringing forward retirement should be something that everyone considers.

Retirement doesn't have to mean an abrupt stop: phased retirement or reduced hours can make the transition smoother and more fulfilling. However, now is the time to prioritize meaningful experiences and family time over further accumulation:

- While working one more year can have a significant financial impact, weigh this against the reality that you may have fewer healthy years left than anticipated.
- As health declines, ensure you have plans in place for healthcare and long-term care.
- If leaving a legacy is important, find the right balance between this and enjoying the fruits of your life's work.
- Transitioning from a career-long focus on wealth accumulation to spending your savings can be difficult. Remember, your retirement pot was built to enable the life you planned. If not now, then when? Embrace it and enjoy!

CONCLUSION: PRACTICAL APPLICATIONS FOR YOUR FINANCIAL INDEPENDENCE JOURNEY

The traditional approaches to career and retirement planning typically lead to a life where two of our resources of time, health, and wealth end up getting prioritized at different times over the third.

The most successful financial independence journeys consider all three and the relationships between them. This can go beyond simple work–life balance and towards work–life optimisation across entire lifespans.

Even the most well-thought-out plan needs occasional revisiting. When doing so it is important to keep the question of whether the balance of time, health, and wealth are where you wanted them to be in your life, and especially in equilibrium over the long term.

In practical terms, this can mean considering the following questions:

- Time: How is my time being spent? What proportion of my time goes towards wealth building for the future and what proportion in experiences and living for today? What proportion is being spent on maintaining my health and my personal relationships?
- Health: Am I focusing on maintaining (or even improving) my physical and mental well-being?
- Wealth: Where am I on "living for today" versus accumulating wealth for the future spectrum?

If we find we do not like some of the answers, we should ask ourselves, "how do I restore the equilibrium?" and then make the financial adjustments that allow us to do so.

The key is not to sleepwalk into finding these choices have been made according to a default, but to create a financial independence journey that focuses on the entire picture – not just wealth but your overall well-being and fulfilment throughout your entire lifespan.

NOTES

1 The interplay between time and wealth is a recurring theme in Perkins's and Ferriss's books. Perkins focuses on making the most of money while we have the time and health to enjoy it, while Ferriss advocates strategies for reclaiming time and challenging the traditional deferred-life model. Perkins, Bill, *Die with Zero: Getting All You Can from Your Money and Your Life* (Houghton Mifflin Harcourt, 2020); Ferriss, Timothy, *The 4-Hour Workweek: Escape 9–5, Live Anywhere, and Join the New Rich* (Crown Publishing, 2009).
2 Smith, Benedict J. and Corfe, Ollie "Revealed: The Age Your Salary Will Peak (It's Earlier Than You Think)" (*The Telegraph*, 7 January 2026). https://www.telegraph.co.uk/money/retirement/age-salary-peaks-how-stop-derail-pension/.
3 Guthrie, Jonathan "Why Our Heirs Need to Inherit Sooner" (*Financial Times*, 13 December 2025), page 4.
4 Mahoney, Paul *The Property Pension Plan: Financial Freedom through Buy to Let Investment* (Rethink Press, 2019), page 10.
5 Kiyosaki, Robert T. *Rich Dad, Poor Dad* (Plata Publishing, 2011), page 235.
6 Burkeman, Oliver *Four Thousand Weeks: Time Management for Mortals* (Farrar, Straus and Giroux, 2021), page 17.

7 Office for National Statistics "Life Expectancy Calculator" (2026). https://www.ons.gov.uk/peoplepopulationandcommunity/healthandsocialcare/healthandlifeexpectancies/articles/lifeexpectancycalculator/2019-06-07.
8 Housel, Morgan *The Art of Spending Money – Simple Choices for a Richer Life* (Harriman House, 2025), page 136.
9 Galloway, Scott *The Algebra of Wealth: A Simple Formula for Success* (Penguin, 2024), page 62.
10 Galloway, Scott *The Algebra of Wealth: A Simple Formula for Success* (Penguin, 2024), page 63.
11 Office for National Statistics "Health State Life Expectancies in England, Northern Ireland and Wales: Between 2011 to 2013 and 2020 to 2022" (2024) (accessed 12 June 2024). https://www.ons.gov.uk/peoplepopulationandcommunity/healthandsocialcare/healthandlifeexpectancies/bulletins/healthstatelifeexpectanciesuk/between2011to2013and2020to2022#:~:text=Healthy%20life%20expectancy%20(HLE)%20at,%2C%2060.3%20years%20for%20females.

REFERENCES

Burkeman, Oliver *Four Thousand Weeks: Time Management for Mortals* (Farrar, Straus and Giroux, 2021).

Ferriss, Timothy *The 4-Hour Workweek: Escape 9–5, Live Anywhere, and Join the New Rich* (Crown Publishing, 2009).

Galloway, Scott *The Algebra of Wealth: A Simple Formula for Success* (Penguin, 2024).

Guthrie, Jonathan "Why Our Heirs Need to Inherit Sooner" (*Financial Times*, 13 December 2025), page 4.

Housel, Morgan *The Art of Spending Money – Simple Choices for a Richer Life* (Harriman House, 2025).

Kiyosaki, Robert T. *Rich Dad, Poor Dad* (Plata Publishing, 2011).

Mahoney, Paul *The Property Pension Plan: Financial Freedom through Buy to Let Investment* (Rethink Press, 2019).

Office for National Statistics "Health State Life Expectancies in England, Northern Ireland and Wales: Between 2011 to 2013 and 2020 to 2022" (2024) (accessed 12 June 2024). https://www.ons.gov.uk/peoplepopulationandcommunity/healthandsocialcare/healthandlifeexpectancies/bulletins/healthstatelifeexpectanciesuk/between2011to2013and2020to2022#:~:text=Healthy%20life%20expectancy%20(HLE)%20at,%2C%2060.3%20years%20for%20females.

Office for National Statistics "Life Expectancy Calculator" (2026). https://www.ons.gov.uk/peoplepopulationandcommunity/healthandsocialcare/healthandlifeexpectancies/articles/lifeexpectancycalculator/2019-06-07.

Smith, Benedict J. and Corfe, Ollie "Revealed: The Age Your Salary Will Peak (It's Earlier Than You Think)" (*The Telegraph*, 7 January 2026). https://www.telegraph.co.uk/money/retirement/age-salary-peaks-how-stop-derail-pension/.

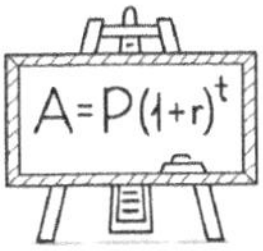

3

FROM PAYDAY TO PROSPERITY

MASTERING CASH FLOW

Ask people what they imagine being a millionaire is like, and many will think about how they would spend a million pounds! That is the quickest way to stop being a millionaire![1] Wealth is the portion of your money that you do *not* spend. Unspent money can be saved and can grow over time via interest, dividends, or capital gains. There is no way around it; effective saving and investing are the building blocks of growing wealth. "There is no such thing as [truly] unspent money … every dollar of savings buys a claim check on your future. (And every dollar of debt … is a piece of your future that someone else controls)."[2]

Many individuals manage money reactively without really having a handle on where their money actually goes. Goals can be quite vague (such as "spend less and save more") with actual savings resulting from whatever is left at month-end rather than from a concrete plan.

We are faced with what in economics we call opportunity cost. Spending today means that we must give up the chance to spend the money on something in the future. It is, therefore, important to be able to work out what money we can spend today without jeopardising what our future self would wish to be able to spend it on.

HOW THE BIG PLAYERS HANDLE BILLIONS IN CASH: THE STRATEGIC ART OF TREASURY MANAGEMENT

Huge multinational companies manage billions in cash daily – they don't do so by hoping for the best or waiting until month-end to discover they have run out of cash. (This approach doesn't really

DOI: 10.4324/9781003792444-3

work for individuals either.) While "cash is king" remains an enduring business maxim (after all, business is all about making money), today's corporate giants must strategically deploy their financial resources to maximise shareholder value, and to ensure the business remains both viable and competitive, in increasingly complex global markets.

Group Treasury departments play an essential role in making this happen – they ensure the company doesn't run out of money while maximising gains on cash surpluses (a high-stakes balancing act that requires precision). It is their role to know where the money is and when it will move, representing the practical application of financial and market theory in managing all aspects of a company's cash and debt portfolio (aligned with strategic corporate objectives).

Treasurers must understand how cash is generated (frequently across the globe in a myriad of separate divisions and group companies) and precisely how and when it will be spent. It is the Treasury department that is responsible for ensuring that the group has the *right amount of money, available in the right place at the right time in the right currency.*

Acting essentially as an internal Group bank, Treasury takes deposits from cash-rich business units around the world and funds those requiring capital. Efficiency demands centralising as much cash as possible in the Treasury department in central HQ. Treasury can then invest the net surplus or borrow to fund a net deficit across currencies.

CASH FLOW FORECASTING

An integral part of being able to achieve the above, and the successful management of liquidity, is the ability to plan ahead.

Treasury departments forecast cash movements by:

- Analysing financial data from accounting systems, ERP[3] platforms, and banking portals
- Incorporating business plans and budgets
- Consulting with internal departments (for example, Accounts Payable for vendor payments, Human Resources for payroll forecasts)

- Studying historical trends, including seasonal variations
- Modelling currency fluctuations and market conditions

This comprehensive process allows the company to profile cash flows and identify the duration of surpluses or shortfalls, enabling Treasury to invest net excess capital, or arrange funding for deficits. The goal is strategically deploying capital to maximise returns without compromising operational flexibility.

Treasurers segment cash and funding into cash buckets by time horizon and purpose. A core component provides day-to-day liquidity, while other reserves might be allocated to medium-term operational needs (e.g. 3–6-month expenses) or long-term growth capital for investments and goals.

The focus is on strategically deploying cash and providing funding to make it work, as efficiently as possible, in the best interests of the long-term aims of the company.

This strategic approach ensures every pound has a purpose – whether covering immediate operational requirements or funding long-term corporate objectives – while optimising capital efficiency across the organisation.

PERSONAL FINANCE PARALLELS

The corporate Treasury model offers valuable lessons for personal financial management. Just as multinational Treasurers track cash flows across global operations to create cash flow forecasts, individuals can monitor income and spending patterns to do the same and develop realistic personal budgets.

To create a personal cash flow forecast – and be able to budget – individuals can begin by looking at and analysing past performance considering the following steps:

- Determine your total take-home pay after taxes and deductions (salary, freelance work)
- Account for irregular income by averaging over time
- Review bank and credit card statements
- Categorise all expenses to identify spending patterns
- Note seasonal variations in your spending (holidays, summer activities)

- Identify fixed expenses (mortgage/rent, insurance) and variable costs (groceries, entertainment)
- Adjust variable expenses to ensure positive cash flow
- Identify potential surpluses or deficits
- Allocate surpluses to savings, investments, or debt reduction
- Over time, analyse variances between projected and actual figures
- Refine future projections based on actual results
- Adjust categories or amounts as your financial situation changes

While corporations use sophisticated ERP systems, individuals can leverage budgeting apps, bank apps, and spreadsheets – or good old pen and paper.

Funds can be allocated to immediate needs (monthly utilities and then building a 3–6-month reserve), medium-term targets (property deposits), and long-term goals (financial independence). This "bucket" approach, borrowed directly from Treasury management, provides clarity and purpose to personal savings and investing decisions.

BREAKING THE PAYDAY-TO-PAYDAY CYCLE

Each of us must balance being spenders versus savers. Building retirement savings requires striking the right balance between living for today and providing for our future selves when we'll rely on the funds we have managed to accumulate. "So many people say, 'oh, I'm not interested in money' yet they'll work at a job for eight hours a day.'"[4]

As Scott Galloway notes in *The Algebra of Wealth*: "'The easiest way to make a dollar is to save a dollar' is good advice. Yet every day … we are confronted with messages, arguments and encouragement to spend."[5]

Our society is built on consumption. There is always the allure of the next must-have product, fashion, or gadget. Financial independence to some extent can involve breaking free from a mindset of consumerism. Financial independence ultimately provides freedom, while consumerism can do the reverse. While we're sold narratives that consumption brings happiness, it can ultimately be experiences, relationships, and personal growth that support genuine freedom; and spending your entire monthly income may indicate overspending patterns that warrant examination.

The crux of it is, living from one payday to the next contains an inherent trap. Throughout a career, our incomes typically rise (through inflation adjustments, we might receive a pay rise as a reward for hard work, reaching our work objectives – or exceeding them – or moving to a higher salary band through promotion). As we build up our experience and climb the career ladder, if our lifestyle is keeping pace with this income growth, we become permanently tethered to the workforce and continually increase our financial requirements.

BUDGETING: THE PERSONAL CASH FLOW STATEMENT

One way of breaking this cycle is establishing that budget – essentially a personal spending plan. Paul Mahoney states in *The Property Pension Plan*: "Budgeting is critical for any household. If you spend more than you earn your finances will be a mess, and you'll get yourself in trouble as this is an unsustainable pattern."[6] Your monthly budget can become your spending limit, requiring trade-offs when priorities shift. The specific rules should depend on your personal discipline requirements.

You know yourself best. If you find it difficult to maintain discipline, physically segregating funds could prove effective – such as transferring your intended savings immediately on payday (paying yourself first) or even setting and establishing direct debits accordingly. Consider opening separate bank accounts for monthly expenditure as well as for guilt-free spending (particularly in the UK where you can open a current account for free).

It can be useful to consider the true cost of your spending in terms of the amount of "life energy" purchases cost you and evaluating them in these terms (i.e. factoring in your real hourly wage by including all work-related expenses and time).[7]

Budgeting serves a purpose far greater than mere expense management. It is also an invaluable tool that not only tracks spending but helps raise financial awareness. Robert Kiyosaki's observation in *Rich Dad, Poor Dad*, that "[c]ash flow tells the story of how a person handles money,"[8] is correct. A budget provides a clear summary of your financial situation: income sources, living costs, but perhaps most importantly it lays your spending habits clearly before you – much like a corporate cash flow forecast. This transparency is particularly useful to identify areas of overspending. Seeing these patterns in black and white can be just the catalyst to make positive adjustments.

The fundamental principle is consistency: either adhere to your monthly budget or understand why adjustments are needed. Without savings, financial freedom remains impossible – you'll depend entirely on whatever state pension or benefit provision exists when you reach retirement age. Whether that proves sufficient for your individual needs becomes irrelevant.

BUDGETING FOR FREEDOM, NOT RESTRICTION

Much of the available financial literature on financial independence planning emphasises techniques to cut expenditure. While living within your means is undeniably necessary, understanding the financial dynamic at work between balancing a budget and "spending versus savings" choices arguably matters more.

In the coming chapters, we'll explore how this awareness forms the foundation of financial independence. Some people may find it initially disquieting to confront their monthly expenditures, but this clarity ultimately can confer a profound sense of control. A budget creates a framework that reinforces saving habits and facilitates long-term planning, but above all, it serves as an accountability tool – the yardstick against which you measure and evaluate financial decisions. Ultimately, having a concrete plan should work to reduce financial stress and not be a source of it.

What matters is understanding your baseline expenditure – your "base case" (the funds you are spending on items such as rent or mortgage, bills, transport, and groceries). It is likely that you will want (or need) to continue to spend at least this level in the future, too. Money you have left after covering your baseline expenditure is the money that is available to be saved and invested – or spent on discretionary items.

In the future, some work-related expenses, for example, may drop away, but you might instead find yourself spending on items you don't currently. There'll be other expenses you are likely to continue. If your social life revolves around restaurant outings with friends several times a week, assuming you'll suddenly cook every meal at home isn't realistic.

Some trimming may be necessary if you are spending unsustainable amounts. Some cuts may come easily – expenses you don't value once examined (subscriptions you rarely use, for instance). However, excessive sacrifice of meaningful life experiences isn't wealth creation – it's deprivation.

Budgeting should address both sides of the equation. You might focus on growing income, extending your timeline for building the asset pools that will fund your lifestyle, or not inflating your expenditure in response to pay rises, for example.

However you choose to do it, pruning expenses or growing income, your timeline to financial independence directly correlates with your savings rate. The shorter your desired timeframe, the greater the emphasis required on saving is.

STRATEGIC ALLOCATION

Adding a savings line item to your budget is simple; understanding what those savings can accomplish is transformative.

If you carry personal debt, such as loans or unpaid credit card bills, allocate specific amounts toward their accelerated reduction. Any monthly surplus should first establish (and maintain) an emergency reserve, ideally equal to 3–6 months of expenses. This fund can cover regular expenses during any income interruptions as well as handling unexpected costs like emergency repairs.

Consider keeping this emergency reserve physically segregated in a dedicated account or very liquid, low-risk investments (such as premium bonds), especially if you might be tempted to dip into this reserve in a "normal" month. Accessibility is paramount; therefore, maintain these funds in cash equivalents rather than investments. In the corporate world, Treasury departments may keep such funds in overnight deposits or money market funds for the same reason.

If you tap this reserve, prioritise replenishing it promptly. Consider maintaining adequate insurance coverage to protect your need to access capital – even during income interruptions that might exceed your emergency fund's capacity.

Additional monthly surpluses should then go towards building your capital base – these represent funds that should arguably never be spent during accumulation, only invested for growth. This capital forms the foundation of financial independence. Therefore, once designated as capital, these funds should remain permanently in your wealth-building system.

One way of achieving this is to create a dedicated savings account for major (non-investment) purchases of depreciating assets (vehicles, holidays, and other big-ticket items) that exceed single-month budget capacity – and then save separately for these purchases via regular monthly contributions until reaching your target.

Since an investment return can't be expected from these types of purchases, using capital for such outlays merely diminishes the power of your investments to compound over time – the engine of financial independence we'll explore in forthcoming chapters. Some level of consistent saving is necessary to build investable funds. Later, we'll also examine the relationship between how much you save and financial independence, laying the foundations for developing a more comprehensive plan that you can tailor for yourself.

For now, understanding spending patterns will give you an indication of where the plan needs to start and to answer the question "what do you want your portfolio to ultimately support?"

The journey from payday dependence to prosperity begins with a fundamental awareness of cash flow at this level – a lesson the corporate Treasury departments of the world's largest companies have long understood and mastered.

NOTES

1 Housel, Morgan *The Psychology of Money* (Harriman House, 2020), chapter 9.
2 Housel, Morgan *The Art of Spending Money – Simple Choices for a Richer Life* (Harriman House, 2025), page 135.
3 ERP (Enterprise Resource Planning) refers to "a type of software that organizations use to manage day-to-day business activities such as accounting, procurement, project management, risk management and compliance, and supply chain operations. A complete ERP suite also includes enterprise performance management, software that helps plan, budget, predict, and report on an organization's financial results." Oracle "What Is ERP?" (no date) (accessed 20 February 2026). https://www.oracle.com/uk/erp/what-is-erp/#:~:text=ERP%20stands%20for%20enterprise%20resource,chain%2C%20finance%2C%20accounting%2C%20and%20more.
4 Kiyosaki, Robert T. *Rich Dad, Poor Dad* (Plata Publishing, 2011), page 45.
5 Galloway, Scott *The Algebra of Wealth: A Simple Formula for Success* (Penguin, 2024), page 19.

6 Mahoney, Paul *The Property Pension Plan: Financial Freedom through Buy to Let Investment* (Rethink Press, 2019), page 43.
7 "How many hours of my life energy will this cost me?" is a key idea from Chapter 3 in Dominguez, Joe and Robin, Vicki *Your Money or Your Life* (Penguin, 2008).
8 Kiyosaki, Robert T. *Rich Dad, Poor Dad* (Plata Publishing, 2011), page 71.

REFERENCES

Dominguez, Joe and Robin, Vicki *Your Money or Your Life* (Penguin, 2008).

Galloway, Scott *The Algebra of Wealth: A Simple Formula for Success* (Penguin, 2024).

Housel, Morgan *The Art of Spending Money – Simple Choices for a Richer Life* (Harriman House, 2025).

Kiyosaki, Robert T. *Rich Dad, Poor Dad* (Plata Publishing, 2011).

Mahoney, Paul *The Property Pension Plan: Financial Freedom through Buy to Let Investment* (Rethink Press, 2019).

Oracle "What Is ERP?" (no date) (accessed 20 February 2026). https://www.oracle.com/uk/erp/what-is-erp/#:~:text=ERP%20stands%20for%20enterprise%20resource,chain%2C%20finance%2C%20accounting%2C%20and%20more.

4

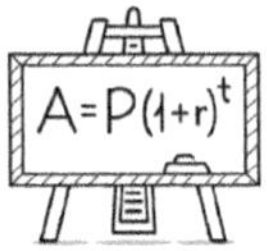

THE MAGIC NUMBER

HOW MUCH IS ENOUGH?

"How much?" (or variations of this) is one of the biggest questions in personal finance and one that most other questions essentially boil down to. Deciding what it means to become financially independent is no different. Here, the "how much" refers to the total amount of money that we need to have accumulated in our pot, so that we can reliably draw funds from it, but not run out of money in our lifetimes.

That is also the question that financial planner William (Bill) Bengen famously sought to answer in 1994. Bengen's study "Determining Withdrawal Rates Using Historic Data" was published in the *Journal of Financial Planning* [1] and has had a transformative impact on independence planning.

Bengen began by analysing historical market data on stock and bond returns over several decades (1926 to 1992). He considered a diversified portfolio that had a stock to (intermediate-term government) bond split of 50:50. He wanted to determine what a safe withdrawal rate from a pension pot would be over a 30-year retirement that would prevent retirees from running out of money.

The idea would be that the initial safe withdrawal percentage (of portfolio value) would be adjusted by the level of inflation in each subsequent year.

Having considered various percentage rates of initial withdrawal, Bengen's research concluded that a 4% withdrawal rate was safe. He found that in "no past case has it caused the portfolio to be exhausted before 35 years." A 4.25% initial withdrawal rate could exhaust the portfolio in 28 years "were past conditions to repeat themselves."[2] Furthermore, "an initial five-percent rate is risky; and six percent or more … 'gambling.'"[3]

DOI: 10.4324/9781003792444-4

Bengen further notes:

> that an "absolutely safe" [rate] (to the extent history is a guide) is 3 percent, in that it ensures that portfolio longevity is never less than 50 years. (This is also true for withdrawal rates as high as approximately 3.5 percent).[4]

In most retirement scenarios this may prove to be very conservative, but not necessarily if we are considering early retirement.

INTRODUCING THE 4% RULE

In practical application, the 4% rule, as it has come to be known, aims to maintain the purchasing power of withdrawals through adjusting the withdrawal rate for inflation.

To implement the rule, a retiree would calculate what 4% of their retirement pot is and withdraw that amount in the first year. They would then adjust the amount the next year by the level of inflation.

EXAMPLE

Gabor has just retired and has amassed a £500,000 pot.

He would be able to withdraw 4% of that, so £20,000, in the first year.

If inflation in the next year was 2.5%, Gabor would increase the withdrawal amount by 2.5% and withdraw £20,500 in the second year, and so on.

CALCULATING THE TOTAL PORTFOLIO SIZE USING WITHDRAWAL RATES

Instead of just relying on the amount we have accumulated in our portfolio to determine the amount we can withdraw, we can take the initiative and adopt a more strategic approach.

If we know the initial amount that we wish to be able to withdraw and knowing the withdrawal rate that we wish to utilise, we can calculate the overall size the portfolio needs to be to support those withdrawals.

Bengen's work helps us understand the impact on our investment pot of different withdrawal rates. For now, let's stick with the 4% rule. The question, then, is to identify the initial amount that we wish to withdraw.

INCOME-BASED APPROACHES TO DETERMINE INITIAL WITHDRAWAL RATES

The Pensions and Lifetime Savings Association (PLSA) publish evidence-based income estimates for UK-based individuals or couples in retirement at three different levels: minimum, moderate, and comfortable. It uses focus groups to research this and is backed up independently by the Centre for Research in Social Policy at Loughborough University. How much relevance this has to your personal circumstances is up to you to decide.

Setting a budget gives you a clear overview of how much cash you, personally, have coming in and going out each month. The financial awareness that gives you might be a better place to start. Using an arbitrary percentage of previous salaried income, or national averages, may bear no relation to how much you really need. The cost of your retirement will be driven by your actual needs and lifestyle choices. Planning based on your adjusted expenses is more useful because it considers your actual financial behaviour.

HOW BIG DOES THE POT NEED TO BE?

The critical question when planning for financial independence is: "How much of our target income needs to come from our investment pot?" To answer this, we must first assess the other income sources available to us.

At the normal retirement age, for instance, the state pension may provide a basic income. Additional sources such as private Defined Benefit pensions, interest, dividends, and rental income might be some others that go, at least, some way to covering a portion of our expenses.

These passive income streams reduce the reliance on our investment portfolio, but it is unlikely that they fully cover all our expenses. The portion of our expenditure that remains uncovered by passive income is what we can refer to as "excess expenditure." This is the amount we need to fund directly from our investment pot.

The formula for calculating excess expenditure is straightforward:

$$\text{Excess Expenditure} = \text{Total Expenditure} - \text{Passive Income}$$

Framing it this way, the question becomes: what is the size of the pot needed to fund "excess expenditure"?

CALCULATIONS REGARDING THE SIZE OF THE INVESTMENT POT

Once we have quantified the monetary amount of "excess expenditure" and established the desired portfolio withdrawal rate, we can calculate the total size of the investment pot required. The formula is simple:

Total Retirement Savings Needed = Annual Excess Expenditure / Withdrawal Rate

EXAMPLE

Let's revisit Gabor's example to illustrate this calculation. Gabor has determined that his annual excess expenditure is £20,000. Using a withdrawal rate of 4% (or 0.04), we can confirm the size of his required investment pot:

£500,000 = £20,000 / 0.04

At a 4% withdrawal rate, this means Gabor needs £500,000 in his portfolio to sustain an initial annual withdrawal of £20,000 (and then be able to adjust it annually for inflation).

You can then check the multiple of how many years' worth of expenses is covered by your current level of savings at any point through the formula:

Total Savings / Annual Expenses

If we do so with the target values at retirement (e.g. in Gabor's case using £500,000 / £20,000), we find that at a 4% withdrawal rate the overall size of the pot needs to be 25 times the annual withdrawal amount (£). This factor can be expressed by simply dividing 1 by 4% (or 0.04).

THE 4% RULE: BENEFITS AND CRITICISMS

Before we go any further, an important distinction to make is that the 4% rule and actuarial drawdown strategies are fundamentally different approaches. The latter is dynamic, flexible, and uses insurance-like actuarial principles to calculate withdrawals – based around age, risk tolerance, life expectancy, portfolio value, and other factors. It is highly personalised (with the advantages that that brings) and market-sensitive, designed to maximise retirement expenditure, while reducing the risk of running out of money. It can require annual recalibrations and withdrawal amounts can vary, potentially making budgeting more challenging.

The 4% rule, meanwhile, has proved popular as a rule of thumb. It is easy to see why: it's simple to understand, for what is otherwise a complex problem, it sets a useful framework for planning purposes, and provides an uncomplicated yet effective way, based on actual historical outcomes, to manage fixed predictable withdrawals. While it is not without criticism, it has been very heavily scrutinised.

Other studies later confirmed and expanded upon Bengen's research, including the well-known Trinity Study. The "Trinity Study of 1998" was conducted by Philip L. Cooley, Carl M. Hubbard, and Daniel T. Walz, who were professors at Trinity University in San Antonio, Texas. Their study found that the median terminal value for stock-dominated portfolios in general increased as the payout period rose – but so did the frequency of portfolio failure (without mid-course reduction in withdrawal rate).[5] The study suggested that a withdrawal rate of 3–4% might provide a higher level of confidence to retirees worried about running out of money.[6]

The Trinity Study, however, confirmed "[m]ost retirees would likely benefit from allocating at least 50% to common stocks," and went on to add "even those retirees who adopt higher withdrawal rates and who have little or no desire to leave large estates may end up doing so if they act reasonably prudent in protecting themselves from prematurely exhausting their portfolio."[7]

Others found the 4% rule might be unduly conservative, such as expert financial planner Michael Kitces, who "did an analysis of the 4% rule going back to 1870 [and] found that it 'quintupled wealth more often than depleting principal after 30 years.'"[8]

The 4% rule, though, is what is now widely used as initial guiderails in financial independence planning, and for ease the calculations in the remainder of this book. It has also been adopted by the FIRE (Financial Independence, Retire Early) movement.

Adherents to FIRE rely on the 4% rule to determine how much they can withdraw from their portfolios over a much longer retirement than what Bengen originally designed it for (sometimes up to 50 years).

It is important to note here that the 4% rate is on the pot's starting value at retirement and doesn't involve an annual recalibration. For example, if in the early years of retirement investment returns are very large and the pot grows greatly in value, the withdrawal rate shouldn't simply be recalibrated by recalculating 4% of the new increased value, because that way we would be following the portfolio up and removing the margin of safety that is baked into the assumptions.

This margin of safety is what compensates for market volatility. In his article, Bengen specifically warned against this scenario, "particularly ... for recent retirees ... not to increase their rate of withdrawal just because of a few good years in retirement. Their 'excess returns' early may be needed to balance off weaker returns later."[9]

MARKET CONDITIONS AND SEQUENCE RISK

One element worth adding to this discussion is the concept of sequence risk – the danger that the timing of withdrawals from a retirement account will damage the investor's overall outcome. This is particularly relevant in the early years of retirement. Market volatility matters. Even if historical average return data remains consistent, encountering an extended period of low returns early in retirement means your portfolio can sustain real damage, potentially compromising the sustainability of your withdrawals. Various remedies and adjustments have been suggested. This can involve dividing portfolios into various buckets for short-term, medium-term, and long-term needs, for example.

Bengen himself considered the impact of alternate asset allocations and says

> holding too few stocks does more harm than holding too many ... confirming what we already know – the superior returns of stocks versus bonds are essential to maximizing the benefit from a portfolio. Too few stocks in the portfolio shortens the minimum portfolio life ... the 50/50 stock/bond mix appears to be the near-optimum for generating the highest portfolio longevity.[10]

He also cautions against increasing the allocation to stocks above 75%, as that accentuates the impact of market dips and "turns out to be counterproductive."[11] A further conclusion that is important to highlight is that "as long as the client's goals remain the same, there is no need to change the initial asset allocation. It is likely to do more harm than good."[12]

SOME FACTORS TO BE AWARE OF

As a starting point, the 4% rule can serve as a useful frame of reference. Approaching its application with flexibility and adaptability can be key. But it can at least help define a target to aim for, which can always be fine-tuned with professional advice to enhance its effectiveness. For our purposes, that is enough.

That said, even if used as a rough guideline, because it uses specific assumptions it is worth lingering on a little longer so that these are fully appreciated.

Firstly, the 4% rule relies on a portfolio composition that is diversified but contains a healthy exposure to equities as well as bonds, and the time horizon examined is specific. Departing from either can require adjustments. For example, a more conservative lower-risk portfolio would run a much greater risk of depleting the pot early.

A longer (or shorter) retirement would lead to retirees needing to adjust their withdrawal rates as well. Put simply, it is not possible to know how long you need your portfolio to sustain itself. People are living longer, and 30 years may well prove too short. This is especially the case if you are planning on retiring early.

Your circumstances and spending patterns may shift – and in fact for many people spending declines through retirement.

Historic rates of return may be very different from the future, or inflation could look completely different, both of which could impact the rule's effectiveness.

PRACTICAL IMPLEMENTATION

Nevertheless, the mathematics of withdrawal rates provides a useful conceptional framework when determining portfolio targets, but successful planning requires ongoing management and adaptation to changing circumstances and market conditions.

A sensible approach might include some of the following elements:

- Use the 4% rule as a starting point, not an absolute when considering targeted portfolio size.
- Consider your personal circumstances – health, longevity expectations, and risk tolerance.
- Factor in all reasonable income sources when calculating your "excess expenditure."
- Consider seeking professional financial advice and personalised planning, which could incorporate actuarial strategies when considering how you actually access your portfolio.
- Regularly review your withdrawal strategy and build in flexibility to adjust withdrawal rates based on market conditions – particularly in the early years of retirement (and don't automatically follow the market up).

SO "HOW MUCH" THEN?

Where then does this leave us in relation to answering the question at the heart of this chapter? The "how much" question. The how big a portfolio should we target question.

Well, if history is any guide, and we adopt the conclusions made by Bengen (and the assumptions underlying his work), we can use the formulas from this chapter to calculate the various portfolio multiples of excess expenditure, to set some rough guiderails.

Using this approach, we arrive at the following:

- At a 3% withdrawal rate, a pot size of 33.33 times the annual level of excess expenditure is "absolutely safe," in Bengen's words (even for a 50-year retirement).
- This is "true also" for a pot of 28.57 times, at a 3.5% withdrawal rate.
- With a pot of 25 times the annual level of excess expenditure (and the 4% withdrawal rate Bengen recommended), no portfolio depletions occurred for 35 years (only) based on history.
- At 24 times excess expenditure, history shows no portfolio depletions for 28 years (at a 4.25% initial withdrawal rate).

- At a 5% withdrawal rate, a pot 20 times excess expenditure would be termed "risky" for a 30-year retirement.
- 17 times excess expenditure, or a 6% withdrawal rate, for 30 years, can be considered to equate to "gambling."

NOTES

1 Bengen, William P. "Determining Withdrawal Rates Using Historical Data" (*Journal of Financial Planning, 7, 4,* October 1994), pages 171–180.
2 Bengen, William P. "Determining Withdrawal Rates Using Historical Data" (*Journal of Financial Planning, 7, 4,* October 1994), page 173.
3 Bengen, William P. "Determining Withdrawal Rates Using Historical Data" (*Journal of Financial Planning, 7, 4,* October 1994), page 179.
4 Bengen, William P. "Determining Withdrawal Rates Using Historical Data" (*Journal of Financial Planning, 7, 4,* October 1994), page 173.
5 Cooley, Philip L., Hubbard, Carl M., and Walz, Daniel T. "Retirement Savings: Choosing a Withdrawal Rate that Is Sustainable" (*American Association of Individual Investors Journal*, February 1998), pages 20–21.
6 Cooley, Philip L., Hubbard, Carl M., and Walz, Daniel T. "Retirement Savings: Choosing a Withdrawal Rate that Is Sustainable" (*American Association of Individual Investors Journal*, February 1998), page 18.
7 Cooley, Philip L., Hubbard, Carl M., and Walz, Daniel T. "Retirement Savings: Choosing a Withdrawal Rate that Is Sustainable" (*American Association of Individual Investors Journal*, February 1998), page 21.
8 Maggiulli, Nick *Just Keep Buying* (Harriman House, 2022), page 91.
9 Bengen, William P. "Determining Withdrawal Rates Using Historical Data" (*Journal of Financial Planning, 7, 4,* October 1994), page 173.
10 Bengen, William P. "Determining Withdrawal Rates Using Historical Data" (*Journal of Financial Planning, 7, 4,* October 1994), page 176.
11 Bengen, William P. "Determining Withdrawal Rates Using Historical Data" (*Journal of Financial Planning, 7, 4,* October 1994), page 176.
12 Bengen, William P. "Determining Withdrawal Rates Using Historical Data" (*Journal of Financial Planning, 7, 4,* October 1994), page 177.

REFERENCES

Bengen, William P. "Determining Withdrawal Rates Using Historical Data" (*Journal of Financial Planning*, 7, 4, October 1994), pages 171–180.

Cooley, Philip L., Hubbard, Carl M., and Walz, Daniel T. "Retirement Savings: Choosing a Withdrawal Rate that Is Sustainable" (*American Association of Individual Investors Journal*, February 1998).

Maggiulli, Nick *Just Keep Buying* (Harriman House, 2022).

5

THE DOUBLE IMPACT OF SAVINGS RATIOS

Your savings rate represents the portion of your disposable income directed toward savings accounts, investments, pensions, and other wealth-building vehicles. "In the long run, it's not how much money you make that will determine your future prosperity. It's how much of that money you put to work by saving it and investing it."[1]

THE FOUNDATION OF FINANCIAL INDEPENDENCE

In the previous chapter, we explored the fundamental question at the heart of achieving financial independence: how to determine when your savings and investments are sufficient to sustain your desired lifestyle without needing to work.

The answer to this question can throw up sums of money that can seem intimidating. This shouldn't be surprising; after all, you're calculating the amount needed to support yourself for decades,[2] potentially 30+ years of retirement, or perhaps even longer in the case of early retirement. Most people will only reach this point after accumulating capital throughout decades of working – from their life's work – and that's just the point. You have an entire working career to amass this amount of money, and you can chip steadily away at the target, one month at a time.

How long it ends up taking isn't bound by notions of where the statutory retirement age is set. Rather, the single most crucial factor influencing your timeline to financial independence is your savings rate. Simply put, the higher your savings rate, the faster you'll achieve your goal.

DOI: 10.4324/9781003792444-5

UNDERSTANDING YOUR SAVINGS RATE

To calculate your savings rate, use this formula:

$$\text{Savings Rate (\%)} = (\text{Amount Saved} \div \text{Total Income}) \times 100$$

For total income,[3] don't forget to add back any pension contributions automatically deducted from your gross pay via salary sacrifice. These contributions are part of your earnings but are directly added to your savings.

EXAMPLE

Suppose your employer contributes £200 to your pension, you save an additional £400 each month (of which £300 is via salary sacrifice and £100 into an ISA), and your monthly take-home pay is £3,000:

Total income: £3,000 + (£200 + £300) = £3,500
Total savings: £200 + £300 + £100 = £600
Savings rate: (£600 ÷ £3,500) × 100 = 17.1%

THE SAVINGS RATIO FORMULA: A POWERFUL INSIGHT

The relationship between your savings rate and financial independence timeline can be expressed through a simple yet powerful formula:

$$\text{Years of work needed to fund 1 year of expenses} = (1.0 - \text{Savings Rate}) \div \text{Savings Rate}$$

Without considering the effects of investment returns, this formula reveals how many years you need to work to save one year's worth of living expenses. It's determined by how much you can (or want to) live on relative to your net income.

The relationship isn't linear – doubling your savings rate from 10% to 20% more than halves the time required.

In general, a 10–15% savings rate (the level usually recommended by financial advisors) is compatible with a normal retirement age.

Table 5.1 The savings rate and financial independence timeline

Savings Rate	*Years Worked Per Year of Financial Independence*
10%	9.0 years
15%	5.7 years
20%	4.0 years
25%	3.0 years
33%	2.0 years
50%	1.0 year
75%	0.33 years

The power of the savings ratio is directly reflected in the multiple of current annual income someone needs to have accumulated to achieve financial independence. The higher the savings rate, the lower this multiple needs to be.

With a 4% withdrawal rate and a 30% savings rate, 70% of your net income will be going on expenses. By multiplying this expense ratio by the factor needed to calculate your financial independence number (i.e. 25 × 0.7), we find you need your portfolio to be 17.5 times the current level of your total net income.

This multiple rises to 22.5 times if the savings rate falls to only 10%, but falls to 12.5 times with a 50% savings rate.

THE DOUBLE IMPACT OF REDUCING EXPENSES

Both sides of the equation matter. By reducing expenses, you simultaneously:

1 Boost your savings rate (more money available to save)
2 Lower the total amount needed for financial independence (based on your reduced expenditure)

This dual effect creates powerful acceleration towards your goal. Permanently decreasing your monthly expenses means you'll have more to save, while simultaneously reducing the target amount needed for financial independence.

Table 5.2 The savings rate and multiple of current annual income

Savings Rate	*Multiple of Net Income Needed for Financial Independence*
10%	22.5 times
15%	21.25 times
20%	20 times
25%	18.75 times
33%	16.7 times
50%	12.5 times
75%	6.25 times

UK HOUSEHOLD SAVING

In the UK, the "household saving ratio …[only] averaged 6.4% from 1955 to 2015, according to the Office of National Statistics."[4] This translates to working 14.6 years to cover just one year's worth of expenses—and, realistically, not all these savings would have been directed toward retirement planning anyway.

Since April 2019, UK law mandates a minimum 8% contribution to pension schemes. While better, this still equates to working 11.5 years to fund each year of retirement – substantially below what most financial advisors recommend.

THE FIRE MOVEMENT

For adherents of the FIRE movement, the goal is maximising the savings ratio to achieve the earliest possible retirement. With a 50% savings rate, for example, every year worked funds one year of financial independence. This mathematical reality drives the movement's emphasis on both increasing income and optimising expenses.

IMPLEMENTING A SAVINGS STRATEGY THAT'S RIGHT FOR YOU

It is one thing to understand the mathematics behind why the savings rate is important and entirely another to implement its principles in the real world. Doing so doesn't have to be paired with a dramatic reduction in quality of life; in fact, it is better if it is not. After all, the key is making incremental changes that it is possible to stick with; otherwise, it is all too easy to roll them back.

Here are some practical suggestions.

LIVING INTENTIONALLY

Implement a "values-based spending plan" (articulated in terms of where you set your budget), rather than across-the-board frugality. Ensure money flows primarily toward your highest priorities – necessities and items that genuinely enhance your well-being. Reduce expenditure on items that don't align with your values, particularly spending to impress others.

When reviewing your outgoings, you might discover that some of your most meaningful experiences cost very little, while certain big-ticket purchases provide minimal satisfaction. This awareness allows you to reallocate resources more effectively, potentially increasing both life satisfaction and savings rate simultaneously.

PAY YOURSELF FIRST

Setting up automated transfers and direct debits immediately after payday can make saving the default rather than something you need to consciously perform – and require ongoing willpower to maintain. This approach removes the decision point each month.

Consider setting up multiple automated transfers to different accounts for different purposes (much like how corporate Treasuries assign each pound to a specific bucket): monthly expenses, debt reduction, emergency fund, short-term goals, and financial independence. This creates a system where money is automatically directed to its intended purpose before you have a chance to spend it.

TAX EFFICIENCY

Maximise the usage of tax-advantaged accounts and strategies (such as utilising salary sacrifice) to effectively increase your savings rate without reducing income. In the UK, this might include maximising pension contributions, utilising ISAs (Individual Savings Accounts), and taking advantage of other tax reliefs available for specific investments.

INCOME OPTIMISATION

Focus on the income side of the ledger by enhancing your earning ability through strategic career moves, personal development, qualifications, obtaining new skill sets, or finding side income streams. While cutting expenses has natural limits, income enhancement often provides a path of less resistance.

HOUSING OPTIMISATION

Since housing typically represents the largest expense category for most households, optimising this area can dramatically increase your savings rate. Consider:

- Downsizing to a smaller property
- Relocating to a less expensive area
- Taking in a flatmate or lodger
- Negotiating rent reductions in exchange for maintenance
- Refinancing mortgages when rates are favourable

SHARING THE RESPONSIBILITY

Involve your partner and family in determining financial goals and finding creative ways to reduce expenses, while maintaining shared experiences and creating memories. Financial independence is rarely achieved in isolation, especially for those with families.

Regular family finance discussions help everyone understand the goals and contribute ideas. Involving children (age-appropriately) has the added benefit of developing their financial literacy and understanding of delayed gratification.

OPTIMISING WINDFALLS

Save a larger proportion of any irregular income such as work bonuses, premium bond winnings (for example, you could simply give instructions whereby any wins are automatically reinvested), and tax refunds. For substantial windfalls like inheritances, consider a "cooling off" period of several months before making decisions, allowing time for emotional processing and thoughtful planning.

GRADUAL IMPLEMENTATION

If you still find yourself needing to cut expenditure, consider the psychological adjustment needed to do this. Moving suddenly can be difficult to maintain. Making changes gradually, say over six months or a year, can significantly increase success rates.

After a period of adjustment, having a higher savings rate may seem like the new normal and life satisfaction can remain stable (or even improve, as being in control of your financial security can be empowering, even while reducing overall expenditure).

While these strategies can dramatically increase your savings rate, accumulating cash alone won't lead to financial independence. Yes, saving is essential but it's only the first step toward financial independence. Saving creates the capital, but it is investing that capital that will transform it into a wealth-generating engine.

INVESTING, NOT JUST SAVING

Frequently, the terms savings and investing can be used interchangeably, but they are not the same thing. A useful way of contrasting the two is they are both steps along the journey towards financial security. Savings represent the essential first step – without savings you will have nothing to invest, unless it is from an external source such as an inheritance.

Investing is transformative – it is what opens the door, not just to wealth preservation, but the growth of capital. When this happens, your portfolio becomes like another earner in your household, one that works around the clock without getting tired, that is, every day the markets are open. At some point in the future, it may become less reliant on your even contributing to it, and its earning power could eventually eclipse yours, thanks to the power of compound growth.

REFRAMING RISK

The common perception that saving is "safe" while investing is "risky" represents a fundamental misunderstanding of financial risk. This view emphasises short-term volatility while ignoring the certainty of long-term purchasing power erosion through holding cash.

Through the lens of long-term financial security, avoiding investment entirely is actually the riskier approach. While cash consistently loses purchasing power to inflation, diversified investment portfolios have historically delivered positive real returns over extended periods, despite short-term fluctuations.

Many savers will have worked very hard and made a lot of sacrifices to boost the amount they have saved. Over the years, I have met many people who have gone to work abroad to provide for their families, for example. They are naturally very cautious about what they have managed to accumulate through their hard work. Many of these diligent savers put money aside but leave it in cash or near-cash instruments, where returns typically don't match inflation. By emphasising saving without the investing part, they are missing a trick – hard work on its own isn't enough to build wealth or (as an old rural saying eloquently puts it) "the donkey would own the farm."

Even modest inflation rates can wreak havoc over savings and steadily erode purchasing power over time. At the UK's target inflation rate of 2%, money loses approximately half its purchasing power every 35 years. If the inflation target is missed and inflation averages 3%, the erosion of purchasing power speeds up dramatically to just 23 years.

Even if cash returns matched inflation (which they rarely do), a 10% savings ratio would still require working 9 years to fund 1 year of retirement expenses. A 45-year career would produce only 5 years of expenditure coverage—leaving retirees heavily dependent on state pensions and able to supplement the income from the state pension by only one-sixth of their pre-retirement expenditure.

BUILDING INVESTING INTO YOUR PLAN

A comprehensive financial plan recognises different types of risk – market volatility, inflation, longevity risk, and opportunity cost. Addressing these various risks actually reduces your overall financial vulnerability compared to relying exclusively on savings.

Beyond simple mathematics, developing a relationship with investing can create a fundamentally different relationship with money. While saving emphasises deferral and preservation (essentially defensive postures), investing fosters a proactive approach to wealth creation. Developing greater financial literacy can extend to other life areas such as career decisions.

Deferring learning about investing can be an easy decision to make but we all lead very busy lives and "most of us are too busy making a living to earn any money."[5] However, understanding basic investment principles can transform your financial trajectory and dramatically accelerate your path to financial independence.

CONCLUSION

Mastering your savings rate forms the foundation of achieving financial independence. What may seem like small incremental improvements can translate into outsized impacts on your timeline. The first step is as simple as reconsidering the priority your future financial freedom has versus your present consumption.

The mathematics isn't complicated, but implementation requires both strategy and determination. By optimising your savings rate and finding the right balance between living for today and providing for your future self, you create the capital that – when properly invested – becomes a powerful engine for your future prosperity.

Remember that financial independence isn't just about the numbers, though – it's about creating options and freedom in your life. Whether you choose to retire early, change careers, work part-time, or pursue passion projects, the financial security you build through disciplined saving and intelligent investing provides the foundation for these choices.

NOTES

1 Peter Lynch cited in Lustig, Yoram *Saving and Investing for Retirement. The Definitive Handbook to Securing Your Financial Future* (Financial Times Guides, Pearson 2016), page 32.

2 This can mean having to create the ultimate budget – one that needs to last from retirement day for the rest of your life. It's another reason getting into the practice of keeping a budget is a good idea.

3 For total income, using your net pay after taxes focuses on disposable income and, therefore, might be preferable for budgeting. However, using gross pay can provide a more comprehensive view and be a better fit for

some modelling. For the latter, some might prefer the formula: Savings Rate = Total Savings / (Total Savings + Expenses) × 100.

4 Lustig, Yoram *Saving and Investing for Retirement. The Definitive Handbook to Securing Your Financial Future* (Financial Times Guides, Pearson 2016), page 29.

5 Hobson, Rodney *Shares Made Simple* (Hariman House, 2018), page 1.

REFERENCES

Hobson, Rodney *Shares Made Simple* (Hariman House, 2018).

Lustig, Yoram *Saving and Investing for Retirement. The Definitive Handbook to Securing Your Financial Future* (Financial Times Guides, Pearson, 2016).

Mr. Money Mustache "The Shockingly Simple Math Behind Early Retirement" (13 January 2012). https://www.mrmoneymustache.com/2012/01/13/the-shockingly-simple-math-behind-early-retirement/.

6

FROM SMALL BEGINNINGS TO BIG OUTCOMES

When I ask many finance professionals whether they'd prefer £1 million today or 1p that doubles every year for 30 years, many choose the million. They're wrong by over £9 million.

At first glance, the question appears so outrageous that even many of those that, correctly, chose the 1p option, conceded that they would have thought a £1 million pot should "of course" be the better choice – but guessed somehow it must "be a trick question." The "trick" is that this example provides a fine illustration of why compound interest (interest upon interest) is such a powerful force given enough time.

Einstein allegedly called compound interest the "Eighth Wonder of the World." Whether or not he actually did, it can transform your financial future.

THE PENNY THAT BECAME MILLIONS

It is difficult to imagine that the result of 1p doubling can win so convincingly. After all, you must wait until the end of the seventh year for the pot just to top £1. It's only in year 14 that it even passes £100. The key insight here is that compound growth starts slowly, appears linear for years, then suddenly explodes exponentially – it is this quality which makes it the "Eighth Wonder of the World."

By the end of year 20, you might still only have £10,486, but this is where the magic starts to happen. By the end of the next year, it's £20,971, then £41,943 the year after.

After 25 years, you reach £335,544, and £671,089 at 26 years.

DOI: 10.4324/9781003792444-6

You hit £1 million during year 27 and finish that year at £1.3 million. But there's still time to go. £1.3 million becomes £2.7 million, then £5.4 million. At the end of 30 years, you would have a staggering £10.7 million!

The complete year-by-year breakdown is shown in Table 6.1.

Before we get too carried away, I hate to be the bearer of bad news, but doubling the value of a portfolio every year is quite a wild assumption. Having said that, our starting point will probably not be just 1p without further contributing to the pot again.

THE RULE OF 72: YOUR QUICK CALCULATION TOOL

We can use a simple rule to understand how long it really takes investments to double at realistic return rates. The Rule of 72 provides a quick way to estimate doubling time. Simply divide 72 by your expected annual return percentage:

$$\text{Doubling Time} = 72 \div \text{Annual Return \%}$$

The higher the interest rate the quicker you will get to your goal.

3% return: 72 ÷ 3 = **24 years** to double
4% return: 72 ÷ 4 = **18 years** to double
5% return: 72 ÷ 5 = **14.4 years** to double
6% return: 72 ÷ 6 = **12 years** to double
7% return: 72 ÷ 7 = **10.29 years** to double
8% return: 72 ÷ 8 = **9 years** to double
9% return: 72 ÷ 9 = **8 years** to double
10% return: 72 ÷ 10 = **7.2 years** to double

EXAMPLE: REAL-WORLD APPLICATION

If Simon invests £10,000 today and expects a 6% annual return, the Rule of 72 tells us his money will double to £20,000 in approximately 12 years.

In 24 years, it will have doubled twice to reach £40,000, and in 36 years, it will have doubled three times to reach £80,000 – all without adding another penny!

Table 6.1 The penny that became millions

End of …	*Total Amount*
Year 1	2p (1p × 2)
Year 2	4p (2p × 2)
Year 3	8p (4p × 2)
Year 4	16p (8p × 2)
Year 5	32p (16p × 2)
Year 6	64p (32p × 2)
Year 7	£1.28 (64p × 2)
Year 8	£2.56 (£1.28 × 2)
Year 9	£5.12 (£2.56 × 2)
Year 10	£10.24 (£5.12 × 2)
Year 11	£20.48 (£10.24 × 2)
Year 12	£40.96 (£20.48 × 2)
Year 13	£81.92 (£40.96 × 2)
Year 14	£163.84 (£81.92 × 2)
Year 15	£327.68 (£163.84 × 2)
Year 16	£655.36 (£327.68 × 2)
Year 17	£1,310.72 (£655.36 × 2)
Year 18	£2,621.44 (£1,310.72 × 2)
Year 19	£5,242.88 (£2,621.44 × 2)
Year 20	£10,485.76 (£5,242.88 × 2)
Year 21	£20,971.52 (£10,485.76 × 2)
Year 22	£41,943.04 (£20,971.52 × 2)
Year 23	£83,886.08 (£41,943.04 × 2)
Year 24	£167,772.16 (£83,886.08 × 2)
Year 25	£335,544.32 (£167,772.16 × 2)
Year 26	£671,088.64 (£335,544.32 × 2)
Year 27	£1,342,177.28 (£671,088.64 × 2)
Year 28	£2,684,354.56 (£1,342,177.28 × 2)
Year 29	£5,368,709.12 (£2,684,354.56 × 2)
Year 30	£10,737,418.24 (£5,368,709.12 × 2)

REALISTIC PORTFOLIO GROWTH ASSUMPTIONS

While our 1p doubling example was dramatic, real-world investing requires realistic expectations. Historical data provides guidance, but it is often stated that past performance is not a guide to future returns. There are good reasons for this.

THE HISTORICAL CONTEXT

Long-term stock market returns have averaged around 7% in real terms and 9–10% nominally annually over decades.[1] However, the latter half of the twentieth century and beyond was an extraordinary period that may not repeat. It has been something akin to a decades-long party driven by post-World War II industrial expansion, the rise of the consumer economy, and the digital revolution. International trade saw a new golden age; capital flowed across borders with ease, leading to the rise and rise of multinational corporations.

The world became integrated as never before, increasing efficiency and driving down cost. Stock markets surged and the US economy reaped an outsized share of the gains. The United States was at the heart of the transformation due to its dominant position in the world economic order.

The collapse of the Soviet bloc ushered in an age of optimism heralded as "The End of History"[2] by some (such as Francis Fukuyama) that sped up globalisation even more. China emerged as a major economic power by utilising its vast labour force to become, in essence, the world's manufacturing hub. It was assumed that this would bring its politics into the capital world order. In practice, it has also brought concerns of intellectual property theft and trade imbalances, but more crucially strategic competition, with altered economic patterns and new geopolitical tensions.

There is growing speculation, and concern, that the future may bring with it fragmentation instead of further integration, with the world possibly fracturing into trading blocks. This would bring with it the return of manufacturing, or if not complete home-shoring then at least "friend-shoring" and protectionist policies, a renewed focus on national security, and the protection of supply chains that could reshape global economic interactions.

Given this backdrop, it might be overly optimistic to use latter twentieth century return averages.

WHY CONSERVATIVE ASSUMPTIONS WORK BETTER

In any case, in terms of planning for financial independence, a principle that stands out is to err on the side of caution. Doing so brings with it a number of benefits:

1. Financial resilience: If your plan works with conservative estimates for returns, you are creating a safety net and anything higher will be a bonus. When you build in this type of contingency, you are setting yourself up for a higher likelihood of success.
2. Lower stress: Why put yourself into a position where you are relying on overly optimistic and aggressive assumptions to meet your goals? High returns go hand in hand with high risks. If your plan requires high returns, you're more likely to follow a higher risk investment strategy than you would otherwise.
3. Flexibility: Conservative planning makes your strategy more adaptable and allows for life's unexpected events without jeopardising your overall financial goals.
4. Pleasant surprises: When markets perform better than expected, you'll be ahead of schedule rather than behind. Any excess returns will come as a pleasant surprise and not be an absolute necessity.

THE PHASES OF COMPOUND GROWTH

To truly get a handle on the power of compound growth, it's helpful to consider three distinct phases. Each phase coincides with a different stage of your financial journey, but considered together they underscore the importance of patience and persistence.

THE CONTRIBUTION PHASE

- Characteristics: Initial progress can appear modest and linear in nature.
- Reality: Most wealth gains result from the contributions made.
- Investment returns: These seem modest compared to contributions.
- Key insight: Keep going; you are building the foundations.

ACCELERATION

- Characteristics: Interest on interest starts to accelerate and match your contributions.
- Reality: The value of your portfolio is starting to grow significantly.
- Investment returns: Growth starts to feel exponential.
- Key insight: Your patience is starting to pay off.

COMPOUNDING EXPLOSION

- Characteristics: Your investment returns start to dwarf the contributions being made.
- Reality: Your portfolio becomes like another earner in your household.
- Key insight: Your portfolio is working harder than you are.

Once the power of your portfolio starts to take over, it begins working around the clock for your long-term prosperity – an earner that will eventually take on most of the work in your financial independence journey.

EXAMPLE: ROSS'S SAVING JOURNEY

Ross saves (and invests) £1,000 and achieves a 5% average annual return.

In the first year, his initial £1,000 contribution earns £50 and ends the year with a total value of £1,050.

In the second year, his original £1,000 contribution earns another £50. However, the first year's £50 interest will generate an "interest on interest" return of £2.50 under its own power (so interest in the second-year totals £52.50).

In the third year, £55.13 total interest is earned.

After 15 years, the total interest earned will exceed the initial capital contribution Ross made.

After 24 years, the interest-on-interest element (alone) will exceed the initial capital contribution Ross made.

PRACTICAL FORMULAS FOR FINANCIAL PLANNING WITH COMPOUND GROWTH

The concept of compound growth is simple yet powerful. Applying it in practice to financial planning, in order to answer real-world questions, such as "how much will a lump sum (or regular investing) grow to?" or, indeed, starting out from a target amount and working backwards to determine how much an initial lump sum, regular investment amounts, or a combination of the two, needs to be requires the use of a few key formulas. Let's explore some of the most useful ones to have in your toolkit.

SCENARIO 1: THE FUTURE PORTFOLIO VALUE WITH A SINGLE INITIAL INVESTMENT

This equation helps you calculate how much a single lump-sum investment will grow to, over time, with compound interest:

$$FV = P(1 + r)^t$$

Where:

FV = future value (the amount your investment grows to)
P = principal (your initial investment)
r = annual rate of return (expressed as a decimal, e.g. 5% = 0.05)
t = time (the number of years the money is invested)

EXAMPLE: SIMON

Simon invests £5,000 expecting 6% annual returns. How much will he have in 20 years?

Step-by-step calculation:

P = £5,000
r = 0.06 (6% as a decimal)
t = 20 years

Therefore:

FV = £5,000 × (1 + 0.06)∧20
FV = £5,000 × (1.06)∧20
FV = £5,000 × 3.207
FV = £16,035.68

Simon's initial £5,000 grows to over £16,000 without any additional contributions.

VALIDATING OUR 1P EXAMPLE

At the outset of the chapter, we considered the compounding effect on 1p of a 100% annual return for 30 years.

We can use the formula to confirm that:

£10,737,418.24 = 0.01 × (1 + 1.00)^30

EXAMPLE: ALISHA

Alisha is trying to reach a savings goal of £10,000. She wants to transfer £5,000 from her cash savings to a Stocks and Shares ISA today and wants to put compound investment returns to work to meet the rest of her goal. In other words, she needs compound investment returns to double her initial contribution.

She uses the rule of 72 to roughly calculate that at a 7% return this should take just over 10 years (i.e. 72 / 7 = 10.29 years).

Alisha uses the compound equation to double-check the exact amount that she would receive as she realises that the rule of 72 is a quick "rule of thumb" approximation.

She confirms that: $5{,}000 \times (1 + 0.07)^{10.29} = £10{,}027.74$.

SCENARIO 2: CALCULATING YOUR REQUIRED INITIAL CONTRIBUTION

Sometimes, you know what your savings goal is but want to work backwards from this to calculate how much you need to invest, today, to reach it.

$$P = FV / (1 + r)^t$$

Where:

FV = future value (the amount your investment grows to)
P = principal (your initial investment)
r = annual rate of return (expressed as a decimal, e.g. 5% = 0.05)
t = time (the number of years the money is invested)

EXAMPLE: SIMON'S PLANNING GOALS

Simon has a savings goal of £16,000 in 20 years' time. How much does Simon need to contribute today if returns are 5%.

Step-by-step calculation:

FV = £16,000 (his goal)
r = 0.05 (5% as a decimal)
t = 20 years

Therefore:

$P = £16{,}000 / (1 + 0.05)^{20}$
$P = £16{,}000 / (1.05)^{20}$
$P = £16{,}000 / 2.653$
$P = £6{,}030.22$

Simon needs to invest approximately £6,000 today to reach his £16,000 goal in 20 years with a 5% return rate.

SCENARIO 3: THE FUTURE PORTFOLIO VALUE WITH REGULAR CONTRIBUTIONS

Given enough time, even modest but regular contributions can build up to substantial wealth. This is why individuals shouldn't wait until they feel they have a meaningful enough contribution to start.

This formula helps you calculate the future value of consistent contributions:

$$FV = PMT \times [(1 + r)^\wedge t - 1] / r$$

Where:

FV = future value (the amount your investment grows to)
PMT = payments (regular annual contribution amount)
r = annual rate of return (expressed as a decimal, e.g. 5% = 0.05)
t = time (the number of years the money is invested)

EXAMPLE: SIMON'S REGULAR INVESTING

Simon contributes £3,000 annually (equivalent to £250 per month) for 20 years at 6% returns. How much will he have in 20 years?

Step-by-step calculation:

PMT = £3,000 (regular annual contributions)
r = 0.06 (6% as a decimal)
t = 20 years

Therefore:

FV = £3,000 × [(1 + 0.06)∧20 − 1] / 0.06
FV = £3,000 × [(1.06)∧19] / 0.06
FV = £3,000 × [2.207] / 0.06
FV = £110,356.77

Simon contributes £60,000 over 20 years but ends up with £110,357 – nearly doubling his money.

SCENARIO 4: COMBINING INITIAL CONTRIBUTIONS AND REGULAR CONTRIBUTIONS

This (complete wealth building) formula captures the dual engines of wealth creation: the power of initial capital and consistent further contributions.

It's particularly useful for those who want to combine a lump-sum investment with regular savings:

$$FV = P(1 + r)^t + PMT \times [(1 + r)^t - 1] / r$$

Where:

FV = future value (the amount your investment grows to)
P = principal (your initial investment)
PMT = payments (regular annual contribution amount)
r = annual rate of return (expressed as a decimal, e.g. 5% = 0.05)
t = time (the number of years the money is invested)

EXAMPLE: SIMON'S COMPLETE WEALTH BUILDING JOURNEY

Simon starts with £5,000 and adds £3,000 every year for 20 years, expecting 6% annual returns. How much will he have in 20 years?

Step-by-step calculation:

Initial investment growth:

FV = £5,000 × (1 + 0.06)^20
FV = £5,000 × (1.06)^20
FV = £5,000 × 3.207
FV = £16,035.68

+

Regular contributions growth:

FV = £3,000 × [(1 + 0.06)^20 − 1] / 0.06
FV = £3,000 × [(1.06)^19] / 0.06
FV = £3,000 × [2.207] / 0.06

FV = £110,356.77

Total Future Value: £16,035.68 + £110,356.77
Total Future Value: **£126,392.45**

Or:

£126,392.45 = £5,000 × (1 + 0.06)^20 + £3,000 × [(1 + 0.06)^20 − 1] / 0.06

Simon contributes £65,000 total (£5,000 initial + £60,000 regular contributions) but ends up with £126,393 – nearly doubling his money.

SCENARIO 5: HOW MUCH MUST I SAVE TO REACH MY TARGET?

This equation helps answer one of the most practical questions in personal finance: "How much must I save each month (in addition to an initial starting balance)[3] to reach my target?"

PMT = [FV − P(1 + r)^t] × r / [(1 + r)^t − 1]

EXAMPLE: SIMON'S RETIREMENT PLANNING

Simon's portfolio is worth £10,000 today and he wants £500,000 in 30 years. With 5% expected returns, how much must he contribute annually?

Calculation:
Future value of initial investment: £10,000 × (1.05)^30 = £43,219
Remaining needed from contributions: £500,000 − £43,219 = £456,781
PMT = £456,781 × 0.05 / [(1.05)^30 − 1]
PMT = £456,781 × 0.05 / 3.322
PMT = £6,876 per year

Simon needs to contribute approximately £6,876 annually (and so about £573 monthly) to reach his goal.

These formulas represent powerful tools for financial planning purposes. Used individually, or in combination, can help you model different scenarios to make informed decisions. Regardless of whether you're calculating how much an investment today, or regular savings, can grow to (combining both), or working backwards from financial targets to inform what your savings rate should be to meet them, these formulas can provide a clear starting point to help achieve your financial goals – and take control of your financial future.

What of those colleagues who chose the £1 million now (versus the 1p with the extraordinary compounding ability, from the start of the chapter)? Well, it turns out they might not have been so wrong after all. Any who would have invested that £1 million (and achieved average historic market returns of 7–10%) would have ended up with between £7.6m and £17.4m themselves after the 30 years.

CONCLUSION

However, the real magic of compounding isn't found just in the numbers but through an appreciation of how small but consistent actions today can create extraordinary outcomes for your future self. This can extend far beyond the financial realm and into other spheres of your life. Your future life is based on the decisions and habits that you form today and persevere with.

Whether you are Simon planning financial freedom, or setting out on a different type of goal, the mathematics we have explored in this chapter can provide a roadmap for transforming even modest contributions into substantial wealth given enough time.

In the next chapter, we'll examine the interplay between savings ratios, growth rates, and withdrawal strategies building on these compound growth principles.

NOTES

1 Siegel, Jeremy J. *Stocks for the Long Run: The Definitive Guide to Financial Market Returns and Long-Term Investment Strategies* (McGraw Hill Education, 2008), page 14.
2 Fukuyama, Francis *The End of History and the Last Man* (Free Press, 2006).
3 The initial starting balance can be the value of your portfolio at the end of the previous year, for instance. As such, this formula is invaluable, during periodic reviews, in recalibrating whether your portfolio is on track to meet your goals, or whether you need to increase contributions.

REFERENCES

Fukuyama, Francis *The End of History and the Last Man* (Free Press, 2006).

Siegel, Jeremy J. *Stocks for the Long Run: The Definitive Guide to Financial Market Returns and Long-Term Investment Strategies* (McGraw Hill Education, 2008).

7

THE FINANCIAL INDEPENDENCE FORMULA

Financial independence might seem like a distant dream for many, but the mathematics behind achieving it can be surprisingly straightforward and accessible. It is essentially the interplay between three key variables – savings rate, investment return, and portfolio withdrawal rate – which determines the rough timeline to your financial freedom. By understanding the dynamics of this relationship, you can chart a course best suited to your individual circumstances and aspirations.

THE TIMELINE TO INDEPENDENCE FORMULA

This "time to financial independence" equation works by calculating how many years it will take until the withdrawal rate from a portfolio equals your desired spending level.

The numerator (top part) calculates how much your portfolio needs to grow relative to your income to support your spending habits.

The denominator (bottom part) accounts for the compounding effect of your investment returns.

The result tells you how long you need to save and invest before you can live off your investments, assuming your spending habits remain consistent – from the power of your portfolio alone. The object is to show 100% self-reliance (and full financial independence) regardless of when you choose to retire[1] (Chapter 19's scenario analysis shows how we can factor the state pension in):

$$T = \ln[1 + (r(1 - s))/(s \times w)] \,/\, \ln(1 + r)$$

DOI: 10.4324/9781003792444-7

Where:

T = Time to financial independence (in years)
r = Return Rate (annual rate of return on investments)
s = Savings Rate (fraction of income saved and invested)
w = Withdrawal Rate (fraction of portfolio withdrawn annually in retirement)
= LN(1 + (Return Rate × (1 – Savings Rate)) / (Savings Rate × Withdrawal Rate)) / LN(1 + Return Rate)

We can rearrange the terms to get:

= LN(1 + (Return Rate × (1 – Savings Rate) × (1 / Withdrawal Rate) / (Savings Rate)) / LN(1 + Return Rate)^2

Step-by-step calculation:

Part I: Inside the first natural logarithm (LN) function:

LN(1 + (Return Rate × (1 – Savings Rate) × (1 / Withdrawal Rate) / Savings Rate)

1. Calculate what you spend (excess consumption)

Example:

If your savings rate is 20%, you are spending 80%.

= (1 – savings rate)
= (1 – 0.2)
= (0.8)

2. Calculate the inverse of the withdrawal rate

The inverse of the withdrawal rate represents how many years of expenses your portfolio needs to support. It is calculated as:

(1 / Withdrawal Rate)

Example:

If your withdrawal rate is 4% (0.04), then:

1 / 0.04 = 25

3. Multiply expense ratio, inverse withdrawal rate, and return rate

Now multiply these three components together to determine the relationship between your spending, portfolio size requirements, and investment growth:

$$\text{Expense Ratio} \times (1\ /\ \text{Withdrawal Rate}) \times \text{Return Rate}$$
$$0.8 \times 25 \times 0.07 = 1.4$$

4. Compare these relationships by dividing them

Divide the result of **Step 3** by the savings rate(s) to adjust for how much of your income you save and invest:

$$1.4\ /\ 0.2 = 7$$

5. Create a growth factor for the logarithm calculation

Add 1 to this ratio:

$$1 + 7 = 8$$

6. Apply the natural logarithm

(The natural logarithm (LN) is a mathematical function that helps account for compounding growth over time).

$$\text{LN}(8) \approx 2.08$$

Part II: For the denominator:

$$\text{LN}(1 + \text{Return Rate})$$

7. Calculate the logarithm of investment growth

$\text{LN}(1 + \text{Return Rate})$
$\text{LN}(1 + 0.07)$
$\text{LN}(1.07) \approx 0.068$

Part III: Final calculation:

8. Divide the results to find years to financial independence

Divide the result of **Step 6** by the result of **Step 7**:

$$2.08 \div 0.068 \approx 30.7 \text{ years}$$

Therefore, in this example, with a 20% savings rate, 7% returns, and 4% withdrawal rate, it would take about 30.7 years to reach financial independence.

Here are some other years to financial independence possibilities (with a 4% withdrawal rate):

Table 7.1 Savings rates and real investment returns

Savings Rate	*Real Investment Return*			
	0%	*5%*	*6%*	*7%*
10%	225	51	46	42
15%	142	43	39	35
20%	100	37	33	31
25%	75	32	29	27
30%	58	28	26	24
40%	38	22	20	19
50%	25	17	16	15

Table 7.1 and Figure 7.1 don't merely show numbers; they reveal possibilities, of what doing the right thing for long enough and consistently enough can achieve. They reveal profound truths about the choices we make and their long-term consequences.

Working to retirement age is not inevitable and that timeline is just one possibility among many. Financial independence is achievable within a reasonable timeframe for many.

Achieving financial independence isn't a matter of luck (such as through winning a large sum of money or receiving an unexpected windfall). Nor is how to achieve it a mystery. It is reached through patience and maintaining discipline.

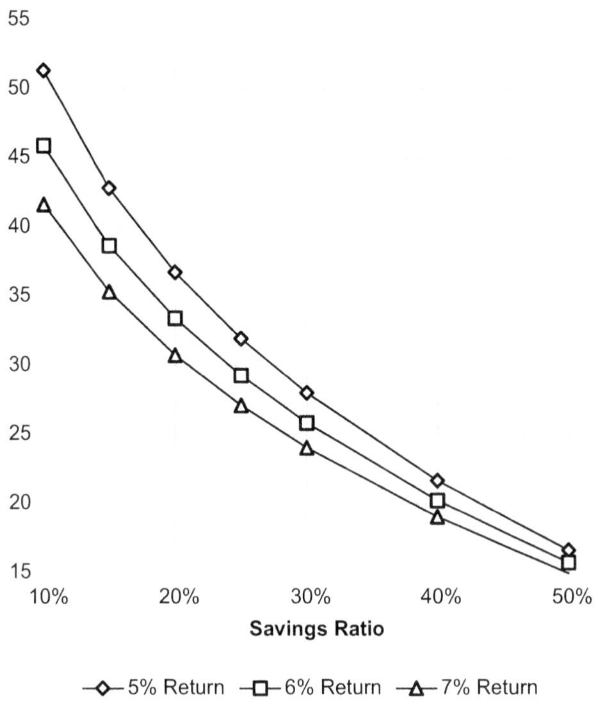

Figure 7.1 Graph showing years to financial independence

INCOME VS WEALTH: CHALLENGING CONVENTIONAL WISDOM

At the same time, the data challenges many conventional wisdoms. Chief among them is that income determines wealth. Wealth accumulation is much more about spending habits and lifestyle. The formula works on a percentage basis and, as such, can be considered independent of actual salary level.

If we understand the concept of wealth as buying time (our freedom), abstract financial inputs are transformed into concrete lifestyle outcomes. The question "how much should I save?" can be transformed into "how many years of my life am I willing to trade for my current level of spending?"

EXAMPLE

If you are choosing to save 15% of your net pay rather than 10%, you are choosing to bring forward the time of your financial freedom by seven or eight years. This trade-off is intuitive. (It is probably obvious to most, for instance, that buying a luxury sports car likely pushes back retirement timelines.)

The percentage saved matters more than the actual amounts involved. A contractor earning £125,000 but saving just 10% will achieve financial independence one and a half to almost two decades later than an analyst on £50,000 who saves 25% – even though both are putting aside £12,500 a year.

That said, it is no doubt easier for someone with higher net pay to achieve a higher savings rate. There is only so much that can be saved by budgeting carefully. Items such as food, transportation, and rent have minimum levels of expenditure attached to them, and this will have an outsized impact on the pocket of someone on the lower income.

WITHDRAWAL RATE IMPACT

Shifting from a 4% to a 3% withdrawal rate extends working years by roughly 15– 20% across most scenarios, and means you will need to accumulate about a third more in assets to support the same nominal annual withdrawal amount. This comes down to a question of personal risk tolerance and conservatism – the increased security comes at the cost of delayed freedom.

Individuals benefiting from passive income such as pensions, rent from buy-to-let properties, or even part-time work opportunities may feel more comfortable with a higher withdrawal rate. It is also possible to use the funds accumulated in a defined contribution pension (or at least a portion) to purchase an annuity if an individual is worried about having to manage withdrawals themselves. The annuity will then pay them a guaranteed regular income.

SAVINGS RATE IMPACT

Increasing your savings rate from 10% to 20% provides a double dividend, in that it does not just double the amount you save, but it also reduces the total amount you need for financial independence by lowering your lifestyle expenses by 10 percentage points.

Increasing your savings rate dramatically reduces the time to financial independence. The steepest acceleration in financial independence timelines occurs when savings rates increase from 20% to 30%, particularly at moderate return levels. This may represent a "sweet spot" in the effort-to-reward trade-off for many households. The timeline to financial independence is dramatically compressed but without needing to compromise as strongly on frugality as with other scenarios.

EXAMPLE

With a 5% investment return, increasing the savings rate from 20% to 30% provides freedom nearly a decade early (after 28 years instead of 37).

The effect with a 7% return is 7 years earlier (24 years instead of 31 years).

Stripping investment returns out of the equation presents an eye-opening scenario that shows that even a 50% savings ratio can still deliver financial independence in 25 years despite having generated no returns whatsoever. (Portfolio depletion in retirement would be a real risk, though, as the 4% rule relies on an investment portfolio with at least 50% in equities.) This scenario beats an investor with a 10% savings rate achieving a 7% annual return by a long way (where a total of 42 years is needed).

This zero-return resilience provides a powerful hedge against the uncertainty of market returns. In other words: a sequence of poor market returns over extended periods can be offset by increasing savings rates, and so individuals can still achieve their financial independence goals.

INVESTMENT RETURNS IMPACT

Compound interest has a far bigger impact the lower someone's savings rate is. In other words, high savers can achieve their financial goals (in effect through brute force) even with more conservative investments than those on a lower savings rate. Paradoxically, low savers are far more reliant on investing wisely to compensate for their savings shortfall.

Without any investment returns, it would take someone starting work at age 18 and a savings rate of 34% of their net pay to reach financial independence (from the power of their savings alone, i.e. assuming no state pension) by the standard retirement age. This timeline is almost halved with a 5% investment return.

With a low savings rate, the power of investment returns becomes quite marked. Without any investment returns: below a 28% savings rate, an individual won't ever achieve financial independence (from the power of their savings alone), unless they live beyond average life expectancy.

EXAMPLE

At a 10% savings rate, financial independence takes 225 years (0% return), 51 years (5% return), 46 years (6% return) and 42 years (7% return).

The benefit of increasing investment returns diminishes at higher savings rates.

EXAMPLE

Going from 0% to 7% return at a 10% savings rate saves 183 years, but at a 50% savings rate saves only 10 years.

Above a 35% savings ratio, returns become significantly less of a variable in determining the timeline to financial independence.

RISK CONSIDERATIONS AND SEQUENCE OF RETURNS

The matrix assumes consistent returns. Sequence of return risk (which assumes that poor returns occur at critical moments) has a surprisingly asymmetrical impact on outcomes. Unsurprisingly, investors with lower savings rates are much more dramatically vulnerable to sequencing risk than those with higher savings rates, even with identical average returns – because investment returns matter more for low savings rate investors. This creates an unappreciated risk factor for moderate savers that standard planning tools rarely address.

If an individual started investing in 1999, they would have encountered two major market crashes within the next decade (the dot-com bubble and 2008 financial crisis). An individual starting a decade later in 2009 would have enjoyed one of the longest bull markets in history. Even with identical savings rates, the variance in investment returns from these two starting points would have delivered differing results.

The compounding effect of even low investment returns can give investors with a high savings rate a compounding benefit, versus those with a lower savings rate but higher returns. This "wealth accumulation cross-over point" is something that many investors don't even consider.

THE BOTTOM LINE

The formula shows the relationship between constant variables. While this can be useful for the setting of guiderails, and during periodic reviews (such as annually), to check if your plan is on track, life may not be quite as neat as the variables assume. It is good, therefore, to be aware of and to consider some of the limitations of such an approach.

For one, future returns may look nothing like history. The often-cited 7% return figure for stock market investments represents a historic average over the long term. However, actual returns over a shorter timeframe can look very different.

Future inflation might erode purchasing power much quicker than allowed for.

Actual life events – ill health, care costs, or unforeseen circumstances – can derail even the best-made plan. We may live far longer than expected, and the portfolio needs to last far longer; after all, the 4% rule considered a 30-year retirement. Taxes could change, pension access could become far more restrictive, or other specific issues could limit the viability of any plan we put together.

Personal circumstances could completely change, spending habits might be different, or it could prove more difficult to maintain overall financial discipline for other reasons. To increase the chances of success, it may be prudent to consult professionals, like an Independent Financial Advisor or Financial Planner, who can consider your specific situation and goals.

CONCLUSION

Nonetheless, the mathematics reveals a few striking conclusions that it is useful for us to take forward:

1 The power of investment returns is most evident at lower savings rates.
2 The impact of increasing your savings rate is profound. In fact, disciplined savings habits may be one of the most undervalued assets in personal finance. Many investors focus on squeezing the most out of investment returns. The challenges of doing so are the focus of some of the forthcoming chapters. There is a reason why those in the FIRE movement emphasise living frugally and boosting savings rates. The analysis of this chapter confirms the impact that accelerating the savings rate can have on the timeline to financial independence.
3 The power of investment returns and a high savings rate can shorten the financial independence journey quite dramatically.

Overall, though, the mathematics of financial independence reveals that this goal is within reach for far more people than conventional wisdom suggests. While the journey requires discipline and consistency, by understanding the powerful interplay between savings rate, investment returns, and withdrawal rate, you can make informed decisions that can potentially shave even decades off your working life. The rewards are profound – not just financial freedom, but the reclamation of your most precious resource: time. Whether your goal is early retirement, career flexibility, or simply greater financial security, the mathematical principles are there to provide you with a roadmap to get there.

NOTES

1 In early retirement scenarios state retirement age might be a long way off and individuals taking it may not qualify fully for a state pension anyway. While the state pension itself is unlikely to disappear, qualification criteria might substantially change (such as needing 35 years of contributions), the retirement age might be lifted, or it could become means-tested – so some individuals may simply prefer not to rely on it when setting a landing area for their portfolios at retirement. This question is also dealt with more fully in Chapter 19.

2 The rearranged formula focuses on multiplying and dividing numbers, making it easier to follow for readers who might prefer straightforward arithmetic. For readers who want to understand the relationships behind financial independence, the original version might provide a deeper, more thoughtful insight into how it works. Both give the same answer.

REFERENCE

Networthify "When Can I Retire?" (no date). https://networthify.com/calculator/earlyretirement.

8

STRATEGIC INVESTING

THE ART OF DIVERSIFICATION

For many, the mere mention of stock markets triggers vivid pictures of risk, volatility, and high-stakes drama. Stock markets might be seen as highly speculative arenas, perhaps not that far removed from gambling, where fortunes can be made (or lost) overnight. Even people unconnected with markets know about the dot-com bubble and the 2008 financial crisis. Headlines designed to sell newspapers, about dramatic market events, crashes, downturns, and significant losses, personal anecdotes about failed investments, popular culture, and the visibility of high-profile investors and hedge fund managers, can combine to leave lasting impressions even on those who have little contact otherwise with the market.

For many, a lack of in-depth financial knowledge then acts to re-enforce these negative stereotypes and ends up in a narrative that can be as misleading as it is intimidating.

"Timing the market each day or week is primarily for short-term traders,"[1] but this overshadows the broader reality that investing is necessary for long-term wealth building. Far from being exclusive playgrounds for professionals, the wealthy, and the financially savvy, when approached with discipline and an informed strategy, stock market investing can (and should) underpin sound long-term financial planning for everyone.

WHAT'S IN YOUR PRIVATE PENSION

Looking under the bonnet of an average investor's portfolio, you'll most likely find a combination of equities, bonds, and cash (with

DOI: 10.4324/9781003792444-8

perhaps a light sprinkling of alternative assets thrown into the mix). Yours, too, if you have a private pension.

A traditional rule of thumb suggests such a portfolio's equity allocation should be 100 minus your age (which leads to a decreasing weighting as you age). This allows for the volatility of markets and the time you have for your portfolio to recover after a downturn.[2]

As Robert Fellowes explains:

> The Age-Adjusted Mix (Variable) ... is designed to change your investment mix from focusing on capital growth in your early years to a more conservative approach whose objective is preservation of capital as you grow older. The formula is 100% minus your age = percentage of assets invested in shares or funds that invest in shares.

An alternative approach is "the Conservative or Balanced mix (40% bonds and 60% shares)."[3]

Meanwhile, as we saw, William Bengen based the 4% rule on a consistent 50:50 split *throughout* retirement. He suggested that if a portfolio has a secondary aim of providing an inheritance to heirs, the split could even be moved to 75:25 in the favour of stocks. However, Bengen found exposures above 75% in retirement could be counterproductive.

The Trinity Study also confirmed:

> the presence of common stocks provides upside potential and holds the promise of higher sustainable withdrawal rates. In other words, the addition of bonds helps increase certainty but at the expense of potentially higher consumption. Most retirees would likely benefit from allocating at least 50% to common stocks.[4]

HISTORICAL EVIDENCE FOR EQUITY ALLOCATION

The reason equity allocations tend to dominate in this manner, quite simply, is equities have outperformed other asset classes over the long term. For example, over 114 years from 1900 to 2013, UK equities outperformed gilts in the majority of cases across examined holding periods. When the holding period was two years, equities outperformed in 68% of cases, and this outperformance generally increased as the holding period did: for three years it was 74%, for five 74%, for ten 79%, and for 18 years 88%.[5]

Globally, we see the same thing during the same 114 years: equities returned an average per annum of 5.2% in real terms while bonds made 1.8%. For the USA the figures were 6.5% and 1.9%, and for the UK 5.3% and 1.4%, respectively.[6]

During a portfolio's accumulation phase, the extended time horizon to weather volatility and benefit from compounding growth makes it worth considering an equity-heavy portfolio, one reason many investment books, including those focused on financial independence, do not concentrate on bonds during this phase.

BUT WHAT DO WE MEAN BY "THE MARKET"?

When you hear "the market" is doing this or that, going up or down, this refers to summary indices of overall market performance. These indicators comprise many underlying shares in individual companies, e.g. the FTSE 100 representing the 100 largest companies listed in London.

Stock market indices are usually weighted. This means that the value of the overall market is determined by calculating the market values (number of shares in issuance multiplied by the share price) of each stock that is a constituent of the index. The result is then divided by the number of shares included in the index. This means that larger companies have a greater impact on the index than companies with less of a market valuation.

Indices are not only a measure of what's happening on a day's trading in the market; they can also be useful over time to pick out trends and market cycles. As such, they act as a benchmark for stock, portfolio, or fund performance.

Averages, such as the Dow Jones Industrial Average (or DJIA) in the United States, are also still used, but indices are usually taken as being the most representative of all market indicators. The DJIA, for example, is unweighted, and each stock price carries equal weight regardless of company value (and contains only the 30 largest companies that mostly represent the older so-called "smokestack" stocks). Today, the S&P 500 is a more common reference point for how the United States (the world's largest stock market) is doing than the DJIA. Its base value was calculated at 10 by averaging the value of the market during 1941–1943. By the end of 2023, its value had soared to an incredible 4,769.83.

Before we move on to consider how you can tap the power of stock market growth, let's first make ourselves more comfortable with stock markets themselves by understanding how they work and the crucial economic functions they perform – as well as the main types of risk that investing in them entails. Finally, let's consider how these types of risks are also inherent in property investing – and why property investing isn't, therefore, a main focus of this book.

INTRODUCING THE ESSENTIAL FUNCTIONS OF STOCK MARKETS

CAPITAL FORMATION

First and perhaps foremost is the role in facilitating the flow of capital. Companies can raise money by issuing shares. The capital thus raised is used for expansion, research and development, and other business uses, all contributing to economic growth. The market also functions as a forum for investors to subsequently buy and sell their shares, providing liquidity.

PRICE DISCOVERY

Through supply and demand (or trading), the market adjusts valuations to reflect all information that is available about the company, including prospects, earnings, and overall market conditions, translating all of this data into a market price (via what is called the price discovery process). In other words, market participants keep buying, or selling, shares until the share price comes to reflect a fair valuation for the company weighing up all that is known about it at the current time.

ECONOMIC INDICATOR

Markets often indicate overall economic health based on the collective opinions of market participants. Publicly traded companies must adhere to reporting and governance standards – ESG (environmental, social, and governance) being increasingly important – leading to better management practices and social responsibility.

RISK DISTRIBUTION

Markets allow investors to spread investments easily (and rebalance their portfolios as and when needed). This enables risk-sharing and serves as a conduit to mobilise savings from individuals and institutions to productive investments. Instead of keeping money idle, it's channelled into businesses that drive the economy.

STOCK MARKET RISK

Stock market risk can broadly be split into two groups: systematic and unsystematic risk.

Systematic risk is the risk inherent in the entire market, commonly called market risk. It's the risk of financial loss from broad-based selloffs. Triggers include global events (e.g. trade wars, and natural disasters like the COVID-19 pandemic), economic factors (e.g. interest rate changes, inflation, recession), and political factors (government policy, political instability).

Meanwhile, **unsystematic risk** (or "specific risk" as it is sometimes called) is associated with specific companies or industries.

Company-level risk factors include company performance, management issues, product recalls, strikes, and operational inefficiencies. Unsystematic risk can arise at industry level as well, such as regulatory changes, windfall taxes affecting entire industries, changing customer preferences, or technological changes.

When buying a share (individual equity), you face both systematic and unsystematic risk (market risk and company-specific risk). Share prices can fall in indiscriminate market selloffs (regardless of individual company performance) or for company-specific reasons even when markets are otherwise buoyant.

Company-specific risk can be diversified away by holding a portfolio of unrelated shares. However, this may require shares in as many as 30–40 different companies, and these will all require active monitoring.

The risk that the overall market will fall (not just a certain share or sector) can't be diversified away – and is therefore sometimes referred to as undiversifiable risk. Even a fully diversified equity portfolio retains systematic risk. Such portfolios function as market trackers (albeit market trackers that might have been costly to acquire). Systematic equity risk can be managed through asset allocation, which is key to properly diversifying a portfolio.

PROPERTY INVESTMENT: AN ALTERNATIVE PERSPECTIVE ON HOME OWNERSHIP AND WEALTH BUILDING

Property, as an asset class, can also play a role here, but there is a simple reason why "most investors should not want to add a property dimension to their … portfolio … via their home, they are likely to have more than enough of their wealth tied up in property" already.[7]

Unsystematic and market risk are also inherent to property investments. Typically, property investments are highly concentrated by definition. If you own your home, a significant portion of your wealth will likely be tied up in a single building, on a single street, in a single city – and potentially highly leveraged if you have low equity relative to asset value. Beyond general property market movements, you face substantial property-specific risk.

THE PSYCHOLOGY OF HOME OWNERSHIP

Many people equate owning their home with financial security. For most, building a deposit to buy their first home is a primary financial goal. When questioned why, many are surprised – to them, the answer seems obvious. "Money spent on rent is wasted as you end up with nothing," they may argue. Interestingly, we don't view money spent on other goods and services in quite the same way. There appears to be something primal about owning our homes.

Many may also add that paying rent is paying off the landlord's mortgage. Yet, arguably, purchasing any good or service might do the same for providers. Vendors might use some of their revenue to pay their mortgages, but this doesn't provoke the same reaction. I'm not arguing against home ownership but suggesting we view its place in our wealth holistically. Owning your home can be a sound financial decision but so can renting and investing the difference.

Rent provides value; we aren't simply throwing the money away. Rent provides a place to live, just as taking out a mortgage and paying interest does. The interest could be viewed as equivalent to rent. After all, both are costs we pay for housing that don't directly contribute to our long-term wealth.

The mortgage cost of owning a property is frequently contrasted with the cost of renting the same property. This isn't usually comparing like-with-like, as there are some additional costs of ownership – such as service charges and maintenance – that you don't pay when you are renting.

In practice, though, before setting foot on the property ladder, many individuals' first port of call is a mortgage broker or bank to ascertain how much they can borrow. Due to transaction costs and the costs of moving, it may seem sensible to try to future-proof a property purchase and plan for the long-term. This approach can translate into buying "more house" than we would opt for if we were just renting for protracted periods.[8] The capital tied up in your home could be working for you elsewhere. This type of lifestyle inflation can prove costly over the long term. The

> years saving money each month ... towards reducing the balance of your mortgage ... could all have been directed towards investments ... as your mortgage balance shrank, the only effect was more protection: you moved steadily closer to the ultimate protection of owning it outright.[9]

HOME AS AN INVESTMENT? ASSETS VS LIABILITIES

Many people *do* consider their home an investment. But unless you plan to downsize in retirement and release equity, there are strong reasons to reconsider this perspective. While there are numerous benefits to owning your home – particularly once mortgages are paid off – you're still left with utilities and maintenance costs. These are liabilities, not assets, and must be factored into your spending plan (just like rent).

Unless you have a lodger, your home generates no income or contribution toward its running costs. For owner-occupiers, the market value is largely irrelevant except for inheritance tax purposes. Whether your three-bedroom semi-detached house rises or falls in value, it remains a three-bedroom semi-detached house.

In *Rich Dad, Poor Dad*, Robert Kiyosaki highlights: "Rich people acquire assets. The poor and middle class acquire liabilities that they think are assets."[10] He defines assets as resulting in cash inflow (putting money in your pocket) and liabilities as having the opposite effect.[11]

Kiyosaki cautions that if all of your money is tied up in your house you may have to work harder. This can have several long-term impacts: you could be mitigating the ability to pay into an investment portfolio, resulting in lost compound growth but also the educational side of the investment experience is lost.[12]

From a financial independence perspective, the primary value of owning property is *potentially* lowering the spending side of the ledger, at least in terms of month-on-month running costs, once your mortgage is paid off. However, it's crucial to consider the overall financial impact, especially if you're climbing the property ladder, and ensure alignment with all your long-term financial goals.

WHY BUY-TO-LET ISN'T ALWAYS THE BEST PATH TO FINANCIAL INDEPENDENCE

In practice, as people become wealthier, many diversify away from property investments. The equity in their homes makes diversification into other asset classes a more sensible choice. The addition of a buy-to-let investment property would concentrate their exposures to property further, maintaining a dangerous lack of diversification (if house prices tank you are impacted both on your primary residence and on your investment properties).

Despite this, many individuals continue to gravitate towards the "real world-ness" of bricks and mortar. They envisage the acquisition of their own home as their first financial priority, then adding buy-to-lets once they can do so, as natural progressions that, together with whatever state pension they would get, would provide passive income, thus taking care of their retirement planning.

Property investing in the UK is not what it once was. Investors face several headwinds.[13] In any case, buy-to-let investments are difficult to scale. They come with substantial entry (and exit) costs – legal fees, survey costs, additional stamp duty, as well as potential capital gains tax charges when selling. These costs can significantly erode profitability. Meanwhile, stock investments have low entry costs, and you can invest small, regular amounts. Stock market portfolios won't phone you saying boilers are broken. It might also be easier to "see why the shares of companies would go up in value: they learn to sell products more cheaply and efficiently over time ... but houses? None of these reasons apply."[14]

At the same time, vehicles like pensions, SIPPs (Self-Invested Personal Pensions), and ISAs in the UK are highly tax-efficient. In the case of pensions, contributions might be made from gross pay, with investments growing tax-free. Whether differences in tax treatment, and other pros and cons, tip scales toward stock investments is for individuals to decide.

From a financial independence perspective, any net income (rent less costs) can be added to the income side of the ledger, with any further excess expenditure needing financing dealt with by the remainder of individual investment portfolios.

The most prudent method of funding remaining excess expenditure is typically balanced portfolios. If primary residences provide security and potential long-term appreciation, augmenting this with stock market investments can offer diversification, liquidity, and truly passive income.

NOTES

1 Sincere, Michael Predict the Next Bull or Bear Market and Win (Sincere Books, 2014), page 16.
2 This type of life styling used to be widespread due to the requirement that private pension funds needed to be used to purchase an annuity in the UK. The rules changed in 2015 and so life styling may no longer be appropriate for many investors as we shall see later.
3 Fellowes, Robert *A Guide to Investing in the Stock Market: The Easyway* (Easyway Guides, 2021), page 158.
4 Cooley, Philip L., Hubbard, Carl M., and Walz, Daniel T. "Retirement Savings: Choosing a Withdrawal Rate That Is Sustainable" (*American Association of Individual Investors Journal*, February 1998), page 21.
5 Arnold, Glen *The Financial Times Guide to Investing* (Pearson, 2014), page 29.
6 Arnold, Glen *The Financial Times Guide to Investing* (Pearson, 2014), page 29.
7 Ryland, Philip "An All-Weather Portfolio" (*Investors Chronicle*, 16–22 September 2022), page 31.
8 In the UK 30% of homes have *two* or more spare bedrooms. Dix, Rob *Seven Myths About Money – And the Truth About Finding Financial Freedom* (Penguin, 2025), page 85.
9 Dix, Rob *Seven Myths About Money – And the Truth About Finding Financial Freedom* (Penguin, 2025), page 85.
10 Kiyosaki, Robert T. Rich Dad, Poor Dad (Plata Publishing, 2011), page 62.

11 Kiyosaki, Robert T. Rich Dad, Poor Dad (Plata Publishing, 2011), page 64.
12 Kiyosaki, Robert T. Rich Dad, Poor Dad (Plata Publishing, 2011), page 83.
13 The regulatory landscape for landlords via successive UK governments is an ever-changing minefield and increasingly complex and costly. The combined effect is to squeeze profit margin greatly. For someone undecided it is worth carefully weighing these up. Not to mention that viewing rent as truly passive income in the way as stock dividends or bond interest can be an illusion. Buy-to-let investments can come with plenty of hands-on work. Day-to-day running can be outsourced but carries ongoing charges (typically 10–15% + VAT for full management). Landlords remain responsible for major decisions and problems even with management companies – tenant selection, property maintenance, legal compliance, and tax management.
14 Dix, Rob Seven *Myths About Money – And the Truth About Finding Financial Freedom* (Penguin, 2025), page 89.

REFERENCES

Arnold, Glen *The Financial Times Guide to Investing* (Pearson, 2014).

Cooley, Philip L., Hubbard, Carl M., and Walz, Daniel T. "Retirement Savings: Choosing a Withdrawal Rate That Is Sustainable" (*American Association of Individual Investors Journal*, February 1998).

Dix, Rob *Seven Myths About Money – And the Truth About Finding Financial Freedom* (Penguin, 2025).

Fellowes, Robert *A Guide to Investing in the Stock Market: The Easyway* (Easyway Guides, 2021).

Kiyosaki, Robert T. *Rich Dad, Poor Dad* (Plata Publishing, 2011).

Ryland, Philip "An All-Weather Portfolio" (*Investors Chronicle*, 16–22 September 2022).

Sincere, Michael *Predict the Next Bull or Bear Market and Win* (Sincere Books, 2014).

9

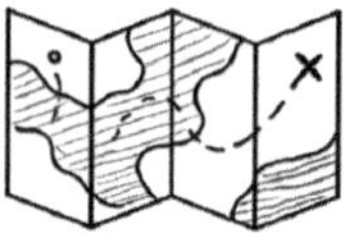

FINDING YOUR INVESTMENT STYLE

Whether to take an active or passive approach to equity investing, or a combination of the two, is one of the most fundamental strategic decisions facing investors. The choice determines not just portfolio construction but heavily influences risk-adjusted returns, cost structures, and complexity.

The active approach is what many associate with stock market investing. It tends to dominate the financial media, with analysis on how to position your portfolio for what is coming next, trying to beat the market through stock selection, strategy, and timing. Passive investing, by contrast, is about capturing market returns rather than trying to beat them.

It isn't merely an academic debate but one that has direct implications for your financial future. Let's explore the key concepts, strategies, and trade-offs that define each approach, starting with two metrics that are central to understanding investment performance: alpha and beta.

THE ALPHA AND BETA OF INVESTING

Alpha measures investment performance against a benchmark index, while beta measures investment volatility against the index.

Active investors who are trying to "beat the market" tend to focus on alpha, while those who are interested in simply replicating market performance, passive investors, would focus more on beta. This fundamental distinction defines the active–passive spectrum.

For active investors, alpha represents the value that is being added to (or taken away) from a portfolio by its manager. Positive

DOI: 10.4324/9781003792444-9

alpha suggests out-performance, i.e. that the portfolio manager has beaten the market average, and negative alpha that the portfolio has underperformed the market index.

Beta can be used to assess how an investment (or portfolio) will respond to a change in value of the whole market. "You might compare Beta to different people's emotional reactivity and expressiveness. Some respond to the slightest good news with outbursts of joy and to the tiniest hardship with wails of despair."[1]

An investment with a beta of 1 indicates that it can be expected to move in line with the market. If the market as a whole gains 1%, the investment would also be expected to gain 1%. As such, it is a measure of systematic risk.

An investment with a beta greater than 1 indicates that it is more volatile than the market, while one with a beta below 1 is less volatile than the whole market.

For example, say ABC Corp. has a beta of 1.1; if the market rises by 1%, the share price of ABC Corp. would be expected to increase by 1.1%. Similarly, if the market were to fall 1%, ABC Corp. could lose 1.1% of its value.

Beta is a useful tool that can be used to assess how much market risk is being taken on with a particular investment. For passive investors, the concern is simply matching market returns and managing risk back to the market. An investment with beta of 1.0 exhibits market-equivalent volatility.[2]

PASSIVE INVESTING

With a passive investing strategy, the aim is to capture market returns. As we saw in the previous chapter, a fully diversified equity portfolio still retains systematic market risk but will have eliminated unsystematic specific risk. Such a portfolio will function as a market tracker.

We can build this ourselves through acquiring enough direct shareholdings. Having said that, such a portfolio would be constructed at considerable cost in selection time, analysis, monitoring, dealing charges, spreads, and stamp duty. A far cheaper, more efficient alternative is simply to buy a fund that acts as a market tracker.

Such a passively managed "index" fund will hold the same stocks in the same proportion as the benchmark index to replicate the performance of that index (or replicate this using derivatives). This is achieved by constantly rebalancing the fund, mechanically, to adjust for share price movements, or when the composition of the index changes. This is automatic as there is no element of judgement involved. (The goal, after all, is simply to mimic the performance of the index.)

If you are content to achieve market returns, there is no need to engage in stock selection, to attempt to identify regions, industries, or individual companies that will outperform the rest of the market – or in trying to time the market. In fact, this approach eliminates discretionary decision-making almost entirely.

Market returns, despite ups and downs along the way, have historically outperformed other investment classes over the long term anyway – and so are deemed adequate by passive investors.

There is a lot to support passive investing for the average investor, not least the simplicity of this strategy. It is straightforward and easy to implement. It doesn't require extensive market knowledge, experience, or constant monitoring.

With an all-equity allocation, a neutral position comprises a single global market capitalisation-weighted index fund. In fact, such a fund can also be used as a benchmark by which to gauge investment performance for active investors seeking to beat the market.

"Tracker funds … [are] for the less adventurous investor who looks for a virtually risk-free return," by which we mean that they only bear systematic risk or, to put it another way, they represent a neutral view towards the market depending on which indices exactly we choose to track.[3]

ACTIVE INVESTING

Active investing entails trying to beat the market, that is, to achieve a higher return than the broader market through a combination of strategies. This can involve stock selection (owning the shares that will perform better than their peers and avoiding those that will underperform) and market timing (selling high and buying low), as well as other techniques.

In practice, this means devoting a considerable amount of time, effort, and resources to analysing company financial statements, accounts, management presentations and other investor communications, market trends, as well as what is happening in the economy.

To take advantage of perceived opportunities, an active management approach is likely to be coupled with frequent buying and selling of undervalued, or overvalued, stocks – or simply to take advantage of market movements.

One thing is for certain: an active approach is not a low-cost approach. The very act of buying and selling will result in transaction costs (broker fees and the spread between buying and selling prices: called "the touch" or bid ask spread). Some brokers now offer free trading for frequent investing, but often they come with the condition that trades are executed once a day. If you are trying to actively time the market, this is likely to be unsuitable, as you lose control over what happens between the time you must give your instruction and deal execution.

If active management works, it has the potential to achieve higher returns. However, this will come with the risk that it relies on skill and market conditions.

As we saw with passive investing, you can buy funds that outsource fund management decisions to a professional fund manager. For active funds, they will need to be compensated for the high costs of research and analysis that they will undertake. Fund management companies employ vast teams to cover the market to identify opportunities, and this will translate into higher management fees.

The management fees are certainly higher when comparing them to a passive approach. Passive funds do not, by their very definition, require extensive research or any active decision-making at all. The fees that passive funds charge will therefore be extremely minimal. Also, passive funds attract a large amount of investors, so can spread the little costs that they do have over a large base, reducing the cost to you.

One thing is for certain: even before you consider returns, active management must make up ground over a passive approach from a fee standpoint. We have seen the power of compounding; it is important to appreciate that costs can compound horribly over the lifetime of a portfolio.

PASSIVE FUNDS, YET ACTIVE MANAGEMENT

Portfolio construction utilising a series of passive instruments does not necessarily constitute a passive investment strategy. This is an important distinction to make.

Consider an all-equity allocation, where the neutral position can be equated to a single global market capitalisation-weighted index fund. The US market, at the end of 2025, will make up the largest country allocation of this, as it does in all major global equity benchmarks. (There are a few competing global indices, but we'll come to that later). Let's say, for now, the US weighting is two-thirds for the purposes of this example.

To gain this level of exposure to the US market, an investor can simply buy the global index fund. Alternatively, they can use two-thirds of the money in their portfolio to buy a US index fund and repeat the process for each other region by buying localised index funds, in the correct proportions, for the remaining third of their portfolio.

In practical terms, divergences between the two approaches are likely to quickly arise as prices move, and due to the precise regional benchmarks selected in the first place (and how rebalancing the portfolio occurs). Index selection introduces active elements: the UK market alone offers multiple alternatives: FTSE 100 (large capitalisation), FTSE 250 (mid-capitalisation), FTSE All-Share (broad market), and AIM (growth-oriented, small-capitalisation). Each of these has distinct risk–return characteristics and sector exposures.

Besides, investors frequently introduce active biases through regional allocation decisions based on performance expectations. Recent US outperformance frequently leads to overweighting this region – versus the allocation inherent in a global index fund. This introduces performance deviation from global market returns, effectively transforming a nominally passive approach into active management, despite implementation through passive vehicles.

Historical perspectives provide a cautionary tale: "at the peak of the Japanese stock market bubble of the 1980s, Japanese shares accounted for almost half the value of all shares."[4] This concentration subsequently experienced dramatic mean reversion, highlighting the risk of geographical overweighting.

The behavioural tendency toward frequent portfolio reallocation can further erode passive discipline. The psychological imperative for action to respond to market movements frequently undermines long-term performance, through poorly timed adjustments, driven by recent performance rather than forward-looking analysis.

ACTIVE INVESTING VS TRADING

There can be an extremely thin line between active management and trading. The principal aim of trading is to profit from short-term price movements, market inefficiencies, and trends. It is a world dominated by agility and emotional detachment. Positions can be held for mere minutes, and an overnight position might even be considered a long-term holding! Decisions are made rapidly and losses closed out without hesitation. Making money is more important than being right and as such trading requires disciplined risk management.

When opening a position, a disciplined trader will begin with clearly defined objectives. Unlike some casual market participants, a professional trader will have carefully considered the economics of each trade before execution. Their preparation extends to identifying a target price as well as defining a stop–loss level at which they will automatically exit the position if the market moves against them.

Crucially, the target price and stop–loss price should not be a symmetrical distance away from the current market price for one. The potential reward from being right about the price movement should greatly exceed the potential loss. For example, a trader risking 1% of his capital may target a 4% gain. If replicating the trade with identical economics four times, the trader only needs to be right 25% of the time to break even. This is a concept known as asymmetric risk–reward. In this example, the reward-to-risk ratio is 4:1. There is nothing magical about a 4:1 ratio other than serving as an example. (I am not suggesting that you randomly target a 4% gain and set a 1% stop–loss.) There is certainly much more to trading than this.

The point is that trading has its own specific rules (I've highlighted one) and they are not the same as for investing. If you are entertaining buying or selling any of your positions (even if they are otherwise passive instruments) to try to take advantage of short-term swings in price, you are making a trade, not an investment; in other words, moving away from the world of active investing and into one of short-term speculation.

That is fine for a trader whose express aim is to capitalise on short-term movements. Show a trader a price chart and they will be able to tell you whether they would be buying or selling without having any further understanding (at all in many cases) of any of the fundamentals of the underlying asset! For an active investor the exact opposite should be true, and indeed such an approach can be fatal. A trader's tools can be driven by "technical analysis," which relies on an assortment of indicators, an understanding of market psychology, and momentum rather than the sophisticated "fundamental" toolkit of a fund manager.

The behaviour required can look very different as well. Rather than seeking to capitalise and "trade" market price swings, a true active investor must frequently hold firm in the face of market sentiment and practise discipline to weather short-term volatility.

Performance may be measured over the *long term* against benchmarks rather than daily or weekly price movements. An active investor invests with the assumption that their investment thesis may take some time to come to fruition; for the market to come around to their way of thinking. It can require a lot of patience. Negative market movements might not result in the dynamic stop–loss techniques utilised by traders, in the face of what might be temporary price movements, but they may represent an opportunity to double-down on convictions at more attractive valuations. (That is not to say that risk management techniques shouldn't be employed; they should.)

Kahneman warns that "many individual investors lose consistently by trading, an achievement a dart-throwing chimp could not match." He cites his former student Terry Odean's study analysing 10,000 brokerage accounts over seven years, focusing on instances where investors sold one stock to buy another. Unfortunately, the stocks they sold outperformed those they bought by "a very substantial margin: 3.2 percentage points per year, above and beyond the significant costs of executing the two trades."[5] In a paper titled "Trading Is Hazardous to Your Wealth," Odean and colleague Brad Barber demonstrated that "on average, the most active traders had the poorest returns, while the investors who traded the least earned the highest amounts."[6]

Consider:

> [An] area that has grown is that of the speculator investor looking for quick returns. Unless you really know what you are doing, then it pays to ... invest for the medium to long term, balancing your portfolio to achieve that aim.[7]

Furthermore: "There are two ways to invest in the stock market, long term (suitable for the small investor) and as an active trader."[8]

Corporate Treasury policies typically prohibit speculative trading activities for sound risk management reasons. Individual investors constructing long-term financial independence strategies may, in many cases, be well advised to adopt similar restrictions, maintaining focus on strategic asset allocation (with passive or active investing) rather than tactical trading opportunities.

CONCLUSION

Investors, depending on their investment goals, risk appetite, time horizon, and beliefs on whether it is possible to beat the market will need to make a call on whether to pursue an active or passive investing strategy. "Your choice between active and passive focuses on three main factors: 1. Your skill in selecting active managers … if lacking skill, go passive and your budget for fees and thirdly, some asset classes 'prefer active management.'"[9]

Passive investment will match (not beat) the market. The "opportunity" cost of this is a lack of flexibility to make tactical adjustments. If you don't have the expertise, interest, or time to manage your portfolio, though, passive investing is practical, some would say ideal.

Michael Sincere in his book *Predict the Next Bull or Bear Market and Win* identifies that "the biggest mistake I made as a beginning trader was not buying an index [fund] … if you're a beginner, start with indexes." He continues: "When you gain more experience, you can use more strategies if you desire. But at the very least, have one broad-based market index in your portfolio."[10] This is sound advice.

Many investors are opposed to basing the equity portion of their investment portfolio only on passive elements through the belief that it is too simple to meet their investment needs or that they should be doing something more complicated.

However, it does not need to be a decision of absolutes, i.e. an either–or decision. It is certainly possible to blend the two. For example, you could use passive investing as a bedrock of the portfolio and layer this with an active element to try and enhance performance. There are some factors that will colour the decision for individual investors, and we will explore these in the coming chapters.

NOTES

1 Paulos, John Allen, *A Mathematician Plays the Market* (Penguin, 2003), page 162.
2 A single equity retains unsystematic risk, even if it historically has displayed a beta of 1.0; how it moves in relation to the market can change going forward.
3 Stone, Robert *Personal Investments* (Straight Forward Publishing, 2022), page 154.
4 Kay, John *The Long and the Short of It* (Profile Books, 2016), page 243.
5 Kahneman, Daniel *Thinking, Fast and Slow* (Penguin, 2024), page 244.
6 Kahneman, Daniel *Thinking, Fast and Slow* (Penguin, 2024), page 244.
7 Fellowes, Robert *A Guide to Investing in the Stock Market: The Easyway* (Easyway Guides, 2021), page 13.
8 Fellows, Adrian *Individual & Family Finances* (Straight Forward Publishing, 2018), page 125.
9 Lustig, Yoram *Saving and Investing for Retirement. The Definitive Handbook to Securing Your Financial Future* (Financial Times Guides, Pearson 2016), page 244.
10 Sincere, Michael *Predict the Next Bull or Bear Market and Win* (Sincere Books, 2014), page 179.

REFERENCES

Fellowes, Robert *A Guide to Investing in the Stock Market: The Easyway* (Easyway Guides, 2021).

Fellows, Adrian *Individual & Family Finances* (Straight Forward Publishing, 2018).

Kahneman, Daniel *Thinking, Fast and Slow* (Penguin, 2024).

Kay, John *The Long and the Short of It* (Profile Books, 2016).

Lustig, Yoram *Saving and Investing for Retirement. The Definitive Handbook to Securing Your Financial Future* (Financial Times Guides, Pearson, 2016).

Paulos, John Allen, *A Mathematician Plays the Market* (Penguin, 2003).
Sincere, Michael *Predict the Next Bull or Bear Market and Win* (Sincere Books, 2014).
Stone, Robert *Personal Investments* (Straight Forward Publishing, 2022).

10

BALANCING RISK AND RETURN

Constructing a portfolio is all about delivering the maximum return for a given level of risk, rather than simply trying to go for the maximum return possible. There is a trade-off between risk and return.

On the first day of my professional career, an old boss of mine (who was the Head of Risk Management at the bank) told me there is an inherent contradiction in what we, as risk managers, would like to achieve – that is, reduce risk to as close to zero as possible; while the proprietary trading team's primary goal is to generate profits for the bank by taking advantage of opportunities in the market. If we were to eliminate risk entirely, the result would be for the trading teams to do "nothing," but that also means that they won't be able to make any money.

The risk management team were focused on what could go wrong, representing the "fear" dimension of investing, while the trading teams represented the "greed" aspect. The two conflicting aims led to an equilibrium, where we tried to control financial risks to within acceptable levels, as determined by senior management's risk appetite, while ensuring the bank's financial stability and adhering to regulatory requirements.

In financial independence terms, "doing nothing" is not a safe strategy. It means that we remain stuck trading our time for money, living from one payday to the next, until there comes a day when we are no longer able to make this trade.

DOI: 10.4324/9781003792444-10

A RISK MANAGEMENT APPROACH

As market risk managers, we had several tools at our disposal for quantifying senior management's risk appetite, which ended up articulated into a hierarchical system of trading limits. A lot of modelling, stress-testing, and back-testing was behind what these limits should be, and they were revisited periodically.

Some underlying parameters, such as value at risk (VaR), could only be calculated on whole chunks of the portfolio. While it was possible to see how much an individual position contributed to the overall portfolio risk figure, it wasn't possible to immediately assess the impact (on overall risk) from adjusting a constituent position, as the overarching calculation took account of the interplay between the underlying portfolio elements, different market rates, and whether these moved together or not.

Limits, however, needed to be easy to understand for traders (and quick in the heat of a busy day on the markets), as you could hardly hold someone to account if they couldn't understand the rules they needed to comply with.

Nominal limits were therefore overlaid and designed so that compliance with these meant a breach of the underlying VaR limit shouldn't happen. (That's one reason why limits needed frequent revisiting to maintain the underlying relationships behind them as rates, correlations, and volatility were all in constant flux.)

At the end of the day, the trading limits articulated the maximum amount of risk that dealers could take while remaining within the bank's stated risk appetite. A limit breach could, therefore, potentially mean financial losses in excess of the risks that senior management thought were being run. Accordingly, each trader would be required to check limits before executing a new trade and normally would be required to immediately reduce the size of positions by entering into offsetting positions, if breaches occurred.

Limit violations had sanctions and trading limits were taken very seriously. Violations were reported up a line of escalation, depending on the severity of the breach, possibly up to the level of various risk committees or perhaps even to the board of directors.

No one wanted to be on the hook for explaining why serious breaches occurred. Traders might even face disciplinary actions and official warnings.

EQUITY INVESTING AS A RISK MANAGEMENT TOOL

In popular perception, equities might be equated to being risky assets due to the inherent short-term volatility in share prices, particularly the shorter the period under consideration. Short-term returns can depart wildly from long-term averages (in either direction), and that is one reason a five-year holding period is considered the minimum in many quarters for stock market investing.

Financial independence, by its very definition, is planning for the long term, whether that is with a decades-long run-up to achieving it or, in the case of extreme early retirements, the duration a portfolio needs to last without running the risk of being depleted.

In relation to both, a healthy allocation to equities in portfolios is an essential risk management tool to have. Equities have historically outpaced inflation over the long term, providing real returns. This is logical, because equities are ownership stakes in companies, most of which could reasonably be expected to be able to adjust the prices of goods and services they provide in the face of inflation. This protects their revenues from the erosion of the real value of money: preserving or even growing purchasing power. Holding investments in them can do the same for your portfolio.

Equities are tied to economic performance, allowing your portfolio to grow in tandem with the economy. The economy itself was viewed by classical economists such as John Stuart Mill and Adam Smith as essentially a productive system driven by human labour.[1]

Via the mechanism of stock market investing, we can, therefore, use the portion of our incomes that we do not consume, but set aside as savings, to invest and profit from a small segment of the global workforce's labour.

The crux of it is that a portion of our individual exchange of time for money goes towards benefiting us when we can no longer make that exchange, from the output of everyone's collective exchange of their time for money, globally.

A conservative portfolio allocation, where a larger proportion of your investments is held as cash and bonds, misses this opportunity for growth, which over the long term can prove costly. A well-diversified allocation to equities in our portfolios, given the potential higher growth returns, puts us in a better place to harness the power of compound growth given the timescales at stake, and reduce the risk that we outlive our retirement savings.

More conservative portfolios give up some of the potential returns and so require a greater starting value in relation to withdrawals. In short, equities are essential for managing inflation and longevity risk.

APPLYING BANKING RISK PRINCIPLES TO PERSONAL INVESTING

In practice, banks (and corporates) accept risk to earn returns. Not managing risk is the riskiest approach, as there is no control over the outcome, and so they are not rewarded for taking on risk.

Individuals can adopt a similar mentality to ensure that their portfolio is aligned with their own financial independence objectives. Setting a **minimum (as well as maximum) equity allocation** limit can be a useful risk management tool to control inflation, longevity, and shortfall risks and means that your portfolio remains exposed to the long-term real growth potential of equities.

SETTING LIMITS: SOME *DOS* AND *DON'TS*

Just as banks periodically revisit trading limits, you can set rules for when you should revisit yours. The overarching principle should be to do so when you can focus on cold hard facts in a detached way. Ideal times are when you are reviewing your financial plan anyway.

Reacting to market conditions (in either direction) can be a bad idea, especially in response to what might well prove to be short-term market "noise." Don't let fear or euphoria dictate what your limits should be adjusted to. In a market downturn, it is natural to feel anxious about losses and potential further losses to come. Similarly, in a "risk-on" mood, it can be tempting to follow the market up.

The point about limit setting is that you should view them as binding on yourself. Consider that your equity allocation should reflect your portfolio's need for long-term growth, but then treat your limits as a trader would treat the limits set by the bank's risk management department.

If it helps, you can mentally borrow my old boss. His name is Gabor. If you are tempted to break the limits you set yourself – when wearing your risk management hat – imagine him holding you to account and asking for an explanation (to be escalated to the risk committee) as to why there has been any limit violation.

THE PURSUIT OF ALPHA WITHOUT CATASTROPHE

A certain amount of diversified equity exposure, then, is desirable to meet our long-term planning goals. The key word is *diversified.* If *beta* calculates our portfolios' sensitivity to market movements (with, as we have seen, a beta of 1 meaning our portfolio moves in line with the market – and so retains market risk but with the company-specific risk eliminated), the more we outperform the market, the higher our portfolio's beta will be (and the higher the risk). That's great if we can consistently beat the market, but there are potentially catastrophic consequences if we are unable to do so and make the wrong calls – or the market moves against us.

Obtaining market-beating returns stems from taking higher risks than the market. Being able to do so consistently over long periods is extremely rare. (There is a good reason for this. If you select a completely random US stock, chances are that it would have underperformed the market.)[2] It's so rare, in fact, that the market is prepared to reward investors who can achieve this richly. Successful high-profile investors have benefited from having something this rare and extraordinary in their possession (enough to be able to beat the sum of everyone else's investing activity over time), and the market has rewarded them with extraordinary wealth for having done so.

There are many who try. Market professionals devote a lot of time, energy, and labour in the pursuit of making a living from the market. Professional firms invest a lot in technological infrastructure. A question to ponder is the amount of effort that you are willing to invest personally. Are you willing to invest more time than average in an attempt to beat the average? Even if you decide yes, understand that from a risk and reward perspective what you are signing up for is the chance to profit from taking on higher risk.

Beating the market by a long way might not be a good thing – even if you manage to do so (and you might not). If your portfolio can depart too wildly from the underlying benchmark, it means it has a high beta value; therefore, if you make the wrong calls, you could lose a lot as well. A sensible area to aim for, if you want to be able to achieve alpha, is to add value but not derail your financial plan by taking too much risk.

It might be an opportune moment to remind ourselves that the stock of time that we have available to trade for money is limited. If we view our portfolios as stores of wealth, the ability for our portfolios to bounce back from catastrophic failures is limited by the amount of time we have left to sell. Taking account of average market returns over time (as we shall see) means understanding that there are periods where the market is crashing as well as enjoying periods of euphoria. Based on history, these have always averaged out well (with markets rising over time) given a long-enough investing period, but this does not take account of the additional value you add (or take away) from your portfolio's performance.

Taking the additional risk might not even be necessary. If you can accept the power of average returns over time, it is far safer to run with the average (i.e. with the market). Anyway, in terms of planning, why develop a plan that forces you to beat the market?

LOW RISK = LOW RETURNS

If all this seems daunting, let us again remind ourselves that trying to eliminate risk translates to low returns. All-cash investors might be able to predict their interest returns with greater accuracy, but over a 40-year stretch "the all-stock investor might finish with 10, 20 or 25 times more capital … if stocks feel like a roller coaster, it may be because you're not looking far enough ahead."[3]

CONCLUDING THOUGHTS

Risk management frameworks exist to keep activities that seek to maximise profits to within "safe" boundaries where the risk and reward trade-off is within overall risk appetite – and, importantly, align with strategic investment goals.

For an investment portfolio, managing longevity and inflation risk is key - and a certain amount of investment in growth assets is necessary for a decades-long retirement. For example, the 4% rule itself assumes a minimum diversified allocation to equities of 50% is maintained throughout. To avoid forcing yourself to take a view on market timing, it makes sense to incorporate a band system of limits: with minimum as well as maximum limit allocations for the assets in your portfolio.

We must also consider how our equity allocations are invested on a risk and return basis. A plan based on average market returns has the power to get us to financial independence without the requirement to force individual investors up the risk versus reward spectrum – and away from a portfolio that is simply diversified in line with the global market. After all, this might be enough for most investors' needs.

NOTES

1 For example, "The annual labour of every nation is the fund which originally supplies it with all the necessaries and conveniences of life which it annually consumes, and which consist always either in the immediate produce of that labour, or in what is purchased with that produce from other nations." Smith, Adam *An Inquiry into the Nature and Causes of the Wealth of Nations* (W. Strahan and T. Cadell, 1776), page 10.

2 Going back to 1963, the median one-year return on individual US stocks is 6.6% but 9.9% for the S&P 500 as a whole. Maggiulli, Nick *Just Keep Buying* (Harriman House, 2022), page 227.

3 Newman, Alex "The Secret to Stress-Free Investing" (*Investors Chronicle*, 30 January–5 February 2026), page 22.

REFERENCES

Maggiulli, Nick *Just Keep Buying* (Harriman House, 2022).

Newman, Alex "The Secret to Stress-Free Investing" (*Investors Chronicle*, 30 January–5 February 2026).

Smith, Adam *An Inquiry into the Nature and Causes of the Wealth of Nations* (W. Strahan and T. Cadell, 1776).

11

YOUR WORST ENEMY IN INVESTING

The start of the working year was signalled by a crisp January day. It was very much a winter's day despite being clear. The sky was blue, the sun was shining, but somehow even the air looked cold. My breath seemed to freeze the instant it was expelled from my nostrils.

I contemplated the start of the year on my way to bank headquarters that morning. It's the time of year for resolutions, but in the world of financial markets, it's also when analysts attempt to predict what various asset types will do in the coming year.

For us working on the trading floor, it also meant the start of a friendly competition. Each dealer would create their dream portfolio with the top five investment picks they thought would perform best for the year. An interesting twist saw each of us also creating a "horror" portfolio with the five investments we thought would *lose* the most money over the coming 12 months.

It was always interesting to see how each dealer would put together their set of predictions. We had a wealth of information at our disposal and were constantly talking to each other, other banks, and corporate market participants about the market. When we got a chance – usually outside normal trading hours – we'd also be reading up on what our house analysts thought and had published, or else engrossing ourselves in news analysis on Bloomberg and Reuters.

THE SURPRISING WINNER

Over time, I observed something highly interesting. Granted, for traders leaving positions open overnight constituted "long-term positions," but most thinking really *was* short-term. We were

DOI: 10.4324/9781003792444-11

particularly good at jumping on momentum and extrapolating recent trends out into the future. As I came to know, there is a name for this type of behaviour: "recency bias."

Things got really interesting as the year ran its course. Some dealers made huge gains, but not from where you might expect. The largest advances, and overall "winner," frequently came from the "horror" portfolios rather than the "dream" tips selection.

What many of the dealers were unconsciously doing, when thinking about selecting their horror portfolios, was looking at already bombed-out assets; the "I wouldn't touch that with a barge pole" type of asset – those that already had significant negative sentiment attached to them. Much of the negative outlook was likely already priced in and so too was potentially a low confidence that the situation was about to improve. With so much bad news in the price, if things turned out less dire than markets expected, prices could bounce quickly.

Those with market knowledge may spot what was happening, a case of "mean reversion" – the theory that holds that assets, given enough time, will return to their average long-run performance. Those going through weak performance periods will eventually move higher, and, crucially, those out-performing, now, may eventually reset (and move back lower to meet their long-term trendlines), much like a stretched rubber band snapping back.

Now, the market has many adages, one being "don't catch a falling knife." So, I'm not necessarily suggesting anyone creates contrarian portfolios of out-of-favour assets (though that is the basic premise of "value investing" – identifying stocks trading below their true worth in the hope that the market comes around to this view).

Prices can fall far more quickly in down markets than they rise in upswings. However, significant bad news can already be allowed for, just as significant good news can be priced into rising markets.

In any case, it's very easy to jump on existing bandwagons in either direction, which is the key danger of "recency bias." But more crucially, even for professional market participants, deciding what investments to pick is difficult. This is the key lesson I took away.

BEHAVIOURAL ECONOMICS

Renowned investor Benjamin Graham famously said that "the investor's chief problem – and even his worst enemy – is likely to be himself."[1]

Neo-classical economics assumes people are rational actors making optimal, well-informed, self-interested decisions based on preferences. However, people in the real world don't behave as economists predict they "should." Combining psychology with economics could explain why. The result is behavioural economics. Adam Smith, as early as the eighteenth century, recognised that people can be over-confident in their abilities and pursue short-term benefits over long-term considerations.[2] This has obvious implications for our overall financial independence journey.

However, there are wider challenges related to this when it comes to investing more generally:

> [P]eople are systematically overconfident tending to put too much faith in their own intuition. Overconfidence in turn is reflected in confirmation bias, whereby we show too ready a willingness to accept as proof any information that reinforces our existing views, and also in self-attribution ... [this leads] to a natural tendency to attribute any disappointment to bad luck rather than a lack of skill.[3]

By definition, this type of selective thinking also means that we may not look as hard at anything that would challenge our held views.[4] The disregarding of some information sometimes only becomes obvious after the fact – after it is too late.

Selective thinking and recency bias are examples of what are called cognitive biases. As an investor, it is also important to be aware of some others.

RUNNING WITH THE HERD

Herding, sometimes called the bandwagon effect, might stem from wanting to fit in, the safety of the crowd, or fear of missing out. For your portfolio, the danger comes from running with prevailing market narratives – collective wisdom knows best – rather than relying on independent analysis or judgement, and a reduction of your individual accountability. For the market as whole, it can lead to collective irrational decision-making and increase systematic market risks.

THE DANGERS OF ANCHORING

One of the more dangerous cognitive biases for our portfolios can be "anchoring." Individuals place unnecessarily heavy reliance on the first piece of information they receive (the "anchor"). Chris Voss in his book discusses how "anchoring" as a technique can be used to achieve the optimal negotiation outcome.[5] In negotiation, I learned that the "loser" is frequently the first to name the "price." This sets the reference point from which negotiation starts, but it's valuable information because it informs you how much something is worth to the person you're negotiating with. That's why tradespeople may ask your budget before indicating their charges.

Anchoring presents real dangers in investing contexts too. If we're anchored to our portfolio's high-water mark, or even individual stock or fund components, we might think in terms of declines from past highs. This can mean reaction times to changing conditions lengthen (it can be difficult to sell "losers," as our need to be right sometimes trumps making money) and could cause heightened stress and anxiety due to market movements.

If we anchored expectations to, say, the previous investment year's end or more historic valuations, we may be more inclined to see the big picture. How much better a story that our portfolio is up 15% versus 12 months ago, as opposed to being down 10% from its recent high-water mark. This is important because the more emotional we get, the greater the chance we make irrational decisions driven by fear rather than cold, rational analysis.

Our portfolios' intrinsic valuations, at least in our heads, are likely tied to our anchors. This means we can overestimate recovery speed, underestimate risk of further losses after sharp declines (opening doors to more stress and anxiety should these not materialise), and disregard new information contradicting our anchored valuations. How many of us have held losing stocks longer than we should have? Talk to any experienced investor and they'll likely admit to this one! Hope may be the last to die and the "disposition effect" sees investors holding losing investments hoping they'll revisit previous highs (or at least purchase values). We must accept that the latest market price is likely a fairer refection of the investment's intrinsic worth rather than our anchored value!

PORTFOLIO MANAGEMENT CONSIDERATIONS

Once portfolios reach certain valuations, it's easy to anchor expectations to them. This presents dangers in areas like recalculating drawdown rates. Say we're using the 4% rule and our portfolio quickly races to new record highs a few years after retirement. Who wouldn't be tempted to re-anchor portfolio valuations and withdraw 4% of the increased valuation? Bengen tested his hypothesis for 4% withdrawals at retirement dates and increasing withdrawal amounts annually by inflation rates. He said nothing about recalculating withdrawal rates after upward movements. (I suspect there wouldn't be as many takers for downward withdrawal rate revisions, except among risk-averse investors.) Not recalibrating makes sense as gains can offset losses in subsequent years and help ensure portfolio longevity.

THE SYMMETRY OF LOSS AVERSION

One of the most formidable obstacles in investing isn't therefore market volatility – it's emotion, specifically the ability to manage your own emotions. Watching the value of your portfolio plummet can trigger profound distress. This could lead you to make expensive mistakes. Behavioural economists have a name for this as well: "loss aversion."

Loss aversion says that the pain of losing money is psychologically more impactful than the pleasure we get from gaining an equivalent amount. The pain from losing £500 hurts more than the joy of winning £500. This can translate into the assumption of greater risk to recover from potential losses than the original risk taken to obtain gains, for instance.

It may seem counterintuitive, but if you are prone to panic and it's going to cause you restless nights, the simplest remedy may be "don't look!" Daniel Kahneman notes:

> Closely following daily fluctuations is a losing proposition, because the pain of the frequent small losses exceeds the pleasure of the equally frequent small gains. Once a quarter is enough and may be more than enough for individual investors. In addition to improving the emotional quality of life, the deliberate avoidance of exposure to

> short-term outcomes improves the quality of both decisions and outcomes. The typical short-term reaction to bad news is increased loss aversion.[6]

This is bad news and is likely over the longer term to make you poorer. As Kahneman continues, "a rational decision maker is interested only in the future consequences of current investments."[7]

The psychological dimension is frequently overlooked in the active versus passive debate as well. Active investing requires emotional discipline, not just the requisite knowledge and skill. Private investors can be more prone to buying high when markets are soaring and selling out at the worst possible time as markets tank and fear takes over.

Higher risk factors:

- Frequent monitoring of investment performance (such as daily)
- Overconfidence in your ability to time the market and to handle losses
- Making decisions based on recent news

Lower risk factors:

- An automated, disciplined approach to investing
- Focus on long-term goals, accepting short-term volatility
- Diversified approach across asset classes

Passive investing can be an antidote to this and at least removes the constant decision-making process. The "behavioural advantage" of passive investing can work well for investors, as even professionals can be prone to emotionally driven mistakes. This can be just as powerful a force as the cost advantage of pursuing a passive strategy.

MANAGING OUR BIASES

Many investors "ride losers and sell winners" due to a combination of the "sunken cost fallacy," loss aversion, and the relief felt from closing successful trades. If we're aware of our biases, we can do something about them. Probably the first step is recognising and calling out what you're experiencing as "cognitive bias." That may be easier said than done. That's why we should ensure portfolios are appropriately diversified and have set asset allocations we're comfortable holding in the long term.

What you want to avoid is emotional, fear-driven decision-making. However, if you're trying to time the market, it's probably because you're being either greedy or fearful. Both of these can be powerful emotions. Given what behavioural economics and cognitive biases have to say, that is important to acknowledge. And if you're being fearful or greedy, are you best equipped at those times with the mental discipline to track markets and act without letting emotions get in the way?

NOTES

1 Value investor Benjamin Graham cited in Lustig, Yoram *Saving and Investing for Retirement. The Definitive Handbook to Securing Your Financial Future* (Financial Times Guides, Pearson, 2016), page 210.
2 Witynski, Max "Behavioral Economics, Explained" (*UChicago News*, no date). https://news.uchicago.edu/explainer/what-is-behavioral-economics.
3 Stanyer, Peter *The Economist Guide to Investment Strategy* (Profile Books, 2016), page 20.
4 Paulos, John Allen A Mathematician Plays the Market (Penguin, 2003), page 21.
5 Voss, Chris *Never Split the Difference* (Penguin, 2022).
6 Kahneman, Daniel *Thinking, Fast and Slow* (Penguin, 2024), page 387.
7 Kahneman, Daniel *Thinking, Fast and Slow* (Penguin, 2024), page 393.

REFERENCES

Kahneman, Daniel *Thinking, Fast and Slow* (Penguin, 2024).
Lustig, Yoram *Saving and Investing for Retirement. The Definitive Handbook to Securing Your Financial Future* (Financial Times Guides, Pearson, 2016).
Paulos, John Allen *A Mathematician Plays the Market* (Penguin, 2003).
Stanyer, Peter *The Economist Guide to Investment Strategy* (Profile Books, 2016).
Voss, Chris *Never Split the Difference* (Penguin, 2022).
Witynski, Max "Behavioral Economics, Explained" (*UChicago News*, no date). https://news.uchicago.edu/explainer/what-is-behavioral-economics.

12

OUTSMARTING THE MARKET

Banks publish extensive amounts of market analysis and insight – as my inbox, at the start of any business day, will testify. Even so, any gaps in coverage can be quickly remedied via our RM,[1] who can link us with any number of the required experts. Even private investors without such privileged access face no shortage of news, commentary, and market analysis. The volume can be overwhelming – and the information often contradictory. This creates a paradox: more information doesn't necessarily lead to better investment decisions. In fact, the constant temptation to react to market news can become destructive, resulting in trading losses, transaction costs, and emotional strain.

INFORMATION OVERLOAD AND MARKET NOISE

DIY investors can easily make mistakes – and most do. The odds aren't stacked in your favour. While skill may be the key determinant of a professional's success, for amateur investors, the mistakes they make will often determine their outcomes more than the brilliant moves they may make.

Skilled participants may be able to capture short-term market inefficiencies and "arbitrage" the market to boost returns. As John Kay notes in *The Long and the Short of It*:

> Traders in the City spend long days dealing in securities, with access to unlimited computing power and extensive data resources. How can you compete with them? You can't, and you shouldn't ... an

DOI: 10.4324/9781003792444-12

> obvious and depressing reason for relying on your own judgement is that most people who offer financial advice to small and medium-size investors aren't much good.[2]

The outsized influence of share tips, rather than fundamental analysis, on private investor trading decisions shouldn't be underestimated either. Many retail investors make decisions based on hot tips or trending stocks rather than rigorous evaluation of business fundamentals. As Sincere outlines, quite simply "most people are terrible stock pickers. Often, they get their stock picks from acquaintances, an article they read, or a know-it-all on a financial television program."[3]

OUTSOURCING ACTIVE MANAGEMENT

Given these challenges, many private investors seek to outsource active management to fund managers. Active management can certainly provide the perception of control, and given the volatility of markets, there is something inherently soothing about feeling in control. We can try to find experienced fund managers who may be less susceptible to the inherent traps of selecting all our underlying investments ourselves. This can throw up its own challenges. How do you go about identifying a fund manager who is genuinely skilled and can consistently outperform the market?

You could of course look at overall past performance, but, as the old adage says, past performance is not a guide to the future.

Some fund managers will have multiple and diverse funds. At any given time, some will probably be overperforming while others underperforming their benchmarks.

How can you separate out a fund manager who simply got lucky in the past from those who do consistently show up? A couple of good ideas in a fund manager's career can make or break a manager's reputation. Maybe they had a great idea in the right place at the right time and let their winners run. But can they consistently come up with great new ideas? "How long would it take to determine if someone is a good stock picker? … try multiple years, and even then, you still might not know for sure."[4]

WHEN SUCCESS BECOMES A BURDEN

Fund manager success has its own consequences. The fund that successful managers manage would attract more inflows from investors and inflate the size of the fund. With a larger portfolio to manage, for individual holdings to continue to provide a meaningful contribution to overall fund performance, the position size would need to increase (perhaps drastically).

This may drive the fund up the market capitalisation scale when it comes to its investments.

EXAMPLE: THE MATHEMATICAL REALITY OF FUND GROWTH

Small fund example:

- Fund size: £100 million
- 1% holding: £1 million investment

Large fund reality:

- Fund size: £10 billion
- 1% holding: £100 million investment

The need to maintain good levels of liquidity will compel the fund to invest in companies with larger market capitalisations, but perhaps also compel the fund to add additional holdings, diluting the fund away from its "best ideas."

A way around this would simply be to limit fund size. In practice, some, particularly those who target small company investments, might do this. However, what this actively means is that funds may close their doors to new investors and would effectively be turning away business, a consequence of which would be that they end up earning lower fees. This is directly against their economic interest.

Instead, the funds may manage to end up so large that the manager's ability to earn returns more than their fees becomes impaired. To fully benefit from the fund manager's skill, therefore, you would need to invest with them before they became well-known.

This isn't the only example of when a fund manager's interests may clash with investor goals either.

FEE STRUCTURE INCENTIVES

Financial advisors and fund managers are incentivised to promote active products due to the higher fees involved. These fees can range from annual management fees and other ongoing charges to performance-based fees. The difference between the fees that active and passive funds charge can easily top 1%. The sums involved in achieving financial independence are not negligible, and a 1% additional charge on the portfolio amount can compound horribly over time.

Some market participants, such as brokers, earn their money in transaction fees and commissions. The money they make is in fees or the spread between the buying and selling prices. They don't care what the market is actually doing, so long as it is doing "something" – specifically that price gyrations are causing people to buy and sell or rebalance their portfolios. If a new trend is emerging, investor greed and the fear of missing out can make it an easy story to sell.

STRUCTURAL CONSTRAINTS

Fund managers' incentives and aims may not align with yours for wholly benign reasons. Funds can and frequently do have underlying themes, biases, or embedded styles. That is why it is important to do your research before investing in them. These might be an integral part of how the fund operates and something that the fund manager is bound to, regardless of what their private opinion might be about the prevailing outlook at a given point in time.

Outperformance might be because an underlying theme is simply having it's time in the sun. But when does a winning streak become a crowded trade? As successful strategies attract more capital, their effectiveness often diminishes through increased competition and reduced opportunities. Fund managers may ride the wave, but they can be wedded to set themes as part of the investment objectives for their fund, and thus be unable to sell out if the trend is ending. Some managers don't even try to predict share price moves but rather look at good companies and hope the market will eventually rerate the stock.

It is important to underline that ultimately "fund managers face lopsided incentives: if they decide to take a different view from the crowds, they will win a few clients if they are successful but lose their jobs if they are not. Much safer to run with the herd."[5]

THE ILLUSION OF SKILL

When looking at active fund management, there is no doubt that survivorship bias influences available statistics to some extent. A number of funds are wound up due to poor performance. "The percentage of funds in each performance quintile 2004–9 surviving to 2014: 1st 84% whilst for the 5th quintile it was a much lower 49%."[6] This means that when we look at historical performance data, we're only seeing the funds that survived, which creates an artificially positive picture of active management success rates.

Daniel Kahneman, Nobel Prize-winning psychologist, offers a sobering perspective on what this can mean in practice in *Thinking, Fast and Slow*:

> A major industry appears to be built largely on an illusion of skill... most of the buyers and sellers know that they have the same information; they exchange stocks primarily because they have different opinions ... the puzzle is why buyers and sellers alike think the current price is wrong. What makes them believe they know more about what the price should be than the market does? For most of them, that belief is an illusion.[7]

"Random events can seem quite ordered,"[8] but despite this, chance can play an outsize role in market fluctuations. Famously, the *Wall Street Journal* ran a series of six-month-long stock-picking competitions between a panel of professional stock pickers (the members of the panel rotated between each iteration of the competition) and random selections made by throwing darts! The experiment was repeated many times and, over the series, although the pros did win, they did so only marginally.[9]

THE ADVANTAGES OF BEING A PRIVATE INVESTOR

Not managing billions means the ability to invest in companies at the smaller end of the scale, or for niche opportunities a large fund would find it impossible to take a meaningful position on. At the same time, funds face redemptions and must account for these by maintaining a degree of liquidity, whereas an individual can commit to their full investment horizon, which for retirement can be decades away.

Fund managers are frequently measured against periodic returns, such as one-year, three-year, and five-year performance against benchmarks. Private investors may have a greater power to maintain contrarian positions, potentially leading to buying when others are fearful and selling when others are greedy if they are able to maintain uncommon emotional discipline.

Professional managers are bound by institutional rules, whether legal or by the investment philosophy of the fund they manage, which could mean an inability to take full advantage of their best ideas or maintain a portfolio diversified to a specified degree.

Private investors face no such constraints and can run much more concentrated portfolios without running career risk. This can leverage genuine information advantages they may have: through specialised professional knowledge, e.g. a software engineer being able to recognise transformative technologies before the knowledge becomes commonplace; through having local knowledge, such as consumer behaviour in specific areas; or simply through being aware of regional trends that have the scope to become more widely adopted.

However, these theoretical advantages come with significant caveats. The freedom to concentrate positions means private investors often move too far up the risk–reward spectrum, which is great if they make the right call but potentially catastrophic if they're wrong. An outsize loss might not only damage their portfolio but could lead them to adopt an unnecessarily conservative approach thereafter, or abandon investing altogether, missing out on long-term compounded gains.

THE PERFORMANCE CHASING TRAP

However, much like with managing a portfolio actively ourselves, which active funds we choose, how we choose them, and when we choose to invest in them are subject to exactly the same cognitive bias traps as selecting underlying investments ourselves. The difference is only that we are buying a part in an already diversified portfolio. We have come full circle.

Investors can easily end up chasing past performance, hoping that this continues. This creates a cycle where:

- Investors identify last year's top performers
- Money flows into these funds
- The funds become larger and less nimble
- Performance often deteriorates
- Investors move to the next hot fund

This aligns with Chris Budd's observation in *The Financial Wellbeing Book*: "The general public more often than not invests emotionally. They tend to go in at the top of a market (when they feel confident) and get out at the bottom (when they panic)."[10]

If this wasn't bad enough, Kahneman adds another behavioural quirk: "Individual investors like to lock in gains by selling 'winners'... and they hang onto their losers."[11] This tendency – selling winners too early and holding losers too long – is directly the opposite of what you should do to mathematically optimise returns.

CONCLUSION

Overall, most professional fund managers will have market insights far more mature than those of average investors. The point is that you simply can't know which ones to back, and that there are many nuances that you will need to consider when moving beyond investing simply in passive funds, and this is key.

Even unusually successful investors, whether professional or amateur, struggle to maintain consistency across all market environments. Truly outperforming involves thinking differently from the herd and having the conviction to act – a rare combination of skills.

Ultimately, the real challenge isn't in finding the next star fund manager but in building a sustainable investment approach, one that considers your individual goals and circumstances unique to you, and that you can have the discipline to persevere with through all market conditions.

NOTES

1 Relationship Manager.
2 Kay, John *The Long and the Short of It* (Profile Books, 2016), pages 2–3.
3 Sincere, Michael *Predict the Next Bull or Bear Market and Win* (Sincere Books, 2014), page 40.
4 Maggiulli, Nick *Just Keep Buying* (Harriman House, 2022), page 143.
5 Harford, Tim *The Undercover Economist* (Abacus, 2007), page 148.
6 Kay, John *The Long and the Short of It* (Profile Books, 2016), page 164.
7 Kahneman, Daniel *Thinking, Fast and Slow* (Penguin, 2024), page 244.
8 Paulos, John Allen *A Mathematician Plays the Market* (Penguin, 2003), page 66.
9 Paulos, John Allen *A Mathematician Plays the Market* (Penguin, 2003), page 63.
10 Budd, Chris *The Financial Wellbeing Book* (LID Publishing, 2023), page 144.
11 Kahneman, Daniel *Thinking, Fast and Slow* (Penguin, 2024), page 246.

REFERENCES

Budd, Chris *The Financial Wellbeing Book* (LID Publishing, 2023).
Harford, Tim *The Undercover Economist* (Abacus, 2007).
Kahneman, Daniel *Thinking, Fast and Slow* (Penguin, 2024).
Kay, John *The Long and the Short of it* (Profile Books, 2016).
Maggiulli, Nick *Just Keep Buying* (Harriman House, 2022).
Paulos, John Allen *A Mathematician Plays the Market* (Penguin, 2003).
Sincere, Michael *Predict the Next Bull or Bear Market and Win* (Sincere Books, 2014).

13

WHY DOESN'T COPYCAT INVESTING WORK?

Stories of successful investors can create the perception that, with the requisite skill and effort, it is possible, consistently, to stay ahead of the market. While these stories can sometimes overlook the role of luck, timing, and survivorship bias, they also serve to highlight the uneven playing field between professionals and individual investors. Professionals have knowledge and resources far beyond the reach of most individuals, making it tempting to outsource parts of our portfolio management in the search of alpha. The challenge is that we then take on having to choose which horses to back. This becomes an even more complex question when considering the construction of an entire portfolio rather than just choosing individual components of it.

PORTFOLIOS OF THE WEALTHY

One approach might be to replicate the portfolios of wealthy investors, if we could find out what's in them. However, this strategy has significant downsides. While wealthy investors' portfolios could very well be built around the same core as that of a typical investor, if they only need to draw on a core of their portfolio (only this part may be invested conventionally). The "core," in some cases, could perhaps even be composed of bond-like investments.

Once wealthy investors have the allocation they need (and have used up ISA and pension contribution allowances to get it), they can afford to be more adventurous with the remainder of their portfolio. This could mean being aggressive with the rest (viewing

DOI: 10.4324/9781003792444-13

it as risk capital), particularly if this part of their funds forms intergenerational wealth, in which case it can be left invested for an ultra-long-term time horizon. The more "exotic end" of their investments might not, then, be suitable for the average investor to copy by any means. That is just the point. Being rich affords someone a margin of safety – a buffer against losses – and as a natural consequence, the wealthy can afford to take greater risks.

Conversely, some might take precisely the opposite view. The priority might be wealth preservation over maximising returns, simply because they have no need to take on that much risk to achieve their purposes.

Regardless of their strategy, it is important to remember that their wealth may not stem from investment skill. We do not know how they got rich. They might not even be good at investing at all. They may simply have been good at the saving part and achieved mediocre returns (and so acted, functionally, as a "drag" on their portfolio in an investment sense). You can still accumulate a decent pot if you have a very high savings rate, or simply an average savings rate but an outstanding salary. Some may have received a good inheritance or have business acumen unrelated to portfolio management.

CASTING A WIDER NET

You could try and cast your net wider and look at investors more generally. The question remains: how would you go about finding them? Finances, in some senses, are one of the last taboo topics. Most people would probably feel uncomfortable discussing them in any detail and there's some good reasons for this.

Meanwhile, other individuals may view investing as a hobby or personal challenge, but this can be dangerous if paired with overconfidence in their ability to beat the market consistently.

Even for those who have made a lot of money from investing, success does not necessarily equal skill – and this doesn't necessarily qualify them to have a special insight into the market. They may not even have a good understanding of investing. "It is often only when the tide goes out that you discover who has been swimming naked."[1] A factor that is often hidden is the risks they took versus the rewards received. It is certainly more than possible that they took horrible risks, and perhaps some of these they were not even aware of – such as running an undiversified portfolio.

They could also have been completely wrong about an idea but the market "let them off," although perhaps that isn't the most likely outcome of being completely wrong when it comes to investing. Their investments might have risen for reasons entirely unrelated to why they bought into an investment in the first place. Would they even know they were wrong? Would they think they were a great investor? Would you?

Naturally, these are all mistakes that any investor could make. Besides, far from letting people off, markets also have an uncanny ability to expose poor risk management.

Being right can be hard enough, but then trying to guess how the market reacts to news requires further nuance. Nick Magulli showed that even if you could "know the future" by seeing forthcoming headlines, guessing the right time to invest is altogether a different thing, because you can't know others' reactions to the news – and so "you're likely to still get it wrong."[2]

There is also a difference between making money from the markets and performing sound analysis. At the end of the day, the market simply does not care about your rationale – and for your portfolio all that counts is investment performance. "You can be right for the wrong reasons or wrong for the right reasons, but to the market you're just plain right or wrong."[3]

A certain degree of humility is always warranted. "Even the smartest, most famous, and wealthiest investors can be completely wrong."[4]

THE MARKET'S ULTIMATE JUDGEMENT

Success in one period is different from consistency over time. Even past consistency doesn't necessarily translate into future outperformance. This truth should be food for thought for anyone weighing up following someone based solely on their reputation or wealth.

Besides, an immediate challenge to outsourcing portfolio management is that you are unique. Your requirements, goals, and risk tolerances are specific to you. Copying someone else's portfolio may not be appropriate for that reason alone.

For default pension funds, try to get around this by creating an investment allocation via a one-size-fits-all approach for individuals who do not wish to actively choose how their pensions are invested, or simply lack the time, knowledge, or interest to engage with this.

DEFAULT PENSION FUNDS

Many such funds follow a so-called "lifestyle" strategy, designed to balance risk and return over time, where the asset allocation gradually shifts away from "growth mode" to an (increasingly) wealth preservation approach, the nearer the holder moves to the statutory retirement age. It achieves this by adjusting (down) the allocation of equities in favour of bonds and other lower-risk assets held in an individual's pension fund. "Life-styling" in this manner was designed to fit with an approach where individuals simply purchased annuities at retirement age.

For individuals planning to break away from the workforce earlier (or later), the default may not reflect your aims – or timeline. A shift into lower-risk assets is unlikely to work for someone comfortable with higher risk – or who should be maintaining (a higher) allocation to equities to manage portfolio longevity or inflation risk. For these, maintaining a certain exposure to growth potential might be desirable. Similarly, conservative investment approaches might not be suitable for individuals with large retirement funding gaps or grand post-retirement aspirations. The default might not allow for strategies or allocations that depart from it.

If you are enrolled in such a scheme, therefore, understanding how your default fund works is essential to be able to assess whether it aligns with your individual requirements. If necessary, you can take control by selecting an alternative investment approach that better aligns with your personal aspirations and risk appetite. Aside from selecting funds and individual assets yourself, which is one method, you could opt to choose an actively managed portfolio that better aligns with your needs – or take financial advice.

FINANCIAL ADVICE

Be aware that many professionals do not want to give you advice. In fact, most will go to great lengths to emphasise that any comments that they do make are their private opinion, guidance regarding factors to consider, rules of thumb, or merely information that may or may not be relevant to your personal circumstances, so should be weighed up by you in that light; the "if it were me" type of thoughts. Most will highlight and highlight again that anything they do say does *most definitely not* constitute financial advice.

A TRADING FLOOR PERSPECTIVE: ADVICE OR MERE OPINION

When I worked on a bank dealing desk, any clients (comprised of dealers in corporate Treasury departments rather than private investors) who asked about what was happening on the markets, at a given time, would typically be given one of two answers (or a combination of both):

1. The house view: What a team of our own analysts thought and had published
2. Subjective opinion: Our own personal view (which we would make clear was exactly what it was)

The latter would be gleaned through watching financial markets all day, having access to an on-the-spot real-time news feed, advanced analytics tools, and discussing the market among us.

We were talking to *professional* clients of the bank, frequently with a deep relationship and all the necessary legal framework that governed it. Any publication of house views also had a robust legal disclaimer at the bottom.

One thing was clear: "these are things to think about" but not financial advice. Even this book isn't advice in that sense. If you want unbiased financial advice related to your own individual circumstances, that is something you will need to pay for. There are good reasons for this.

WHY *UNBIASED* PROFESSIONAL ADVICE COSTS MONEY

A professional owes you a duty of care, which is part and parcel of what you are paying for. They will also be regulated, members of professional bodies, have the requisite qualifications, and a licence to practise, including any relevant indemnity insurance. That is also part of what you are paying for.

If you are uncertain about managing your portfolio, professional financial advice can be invaluable. Such professionals can perform a comprehensive analysis of your personal circumstances as well as offer ongoing monitoring, stress-testing, and portfolio adjustment as needed. Their advice can extend to tax optimisation strategies, risk tolerance assessment, and estate planning considerations and is worth paying for.

CONCLUSION: THE WISDOM OF SYSTEMATIC APPROACHES

On the journey to financial independence, the power of being consistent, and even boring, can rack up impressive results that compound over time – often beating seemingly more sophisticated, clever, and exciting approaches. It's not about finding a successful investor or investment guru to copy. In this sense, the most successful "rich friend" that you can have is a well-diversified low-cost portfolio that you can regularly contribute to. Avoid chasing success stories or investment gurus and concentrate instead on a structured approach, which can compound your investments over time, to reach your financial goals.

NOTES

1 Warren Buffet Archive "You Don't Find Out Who's Been Swimming Naked Until the Tide Goes Out" (25 April 1994) (accessed 20 March 2026). https://buffett.cnbc.com/video/1994/04/25/buffett-you-dont-find-out-whos-been-swimming-naked-until-the-tide-goes-out.html.
2 Maggiulli, Nick "Why You Can't Time the Market (Even When You Know the Future)" (*Of Dollars and Data*, 20 January 2026) (accessed 6 March 2026). https://ofdollarsanddata.com/why-you-cant-time-the-market-even-when-you-know-the-future/.
3 Paulos, John Allen *A Mathematician Plays the Market* (Penguin, 2003), page 5.
4 Sincere, Michael *Predict the Next Bull or Bear Market and Win* (Sincere Books, 2014), page 89.

REFERENCES

Maggiulli, Nick "Why You Can't Time the Market (Even When You Know the Future)" (*Of Dollars and Data*, 20 January 2026) (accessed 6 March

2026). https://ofdollarsanddata.com/why-you-cant-time-the-market-even-when-you-know-the-future/.

Paulos, John Allen *A Mathematician Plays the Market*" (Penguin, 2003).

Sincere, Michael *Predict the Next Bull or Bear Market and Win* (Sincere Books, 2014).

Warren Buffet Archive "You Don't Find Out Who's Been Swimming Naked Until the Tide Goes Out" (25 April 1994) (accessed 20 March 2026). https://buffett.cnbc.com/video/1994/04/25/buffett-you-dont-find-out-whos-been-swimming-naked-until-the-tide-goes-out.html.

14

WHAT YOU SHOULD KNOW ABOUT MARKET EFFICIENCY

Trying to time the market – buying when stocks are cheap, selling after they've risen (buy low, sell high) – is a tantalising opportunity for investors to maximise returns. How great would it be if you could eliminate market cyclicality from your portfolio and profit substantially from it at the same time?

If you could predict when markets were about to fall, you could sell stocks and buy back after they've fallen, avoiding significant losses. You could then buy back stocks ahead of the pack before markets start rising again and make substantial profits.

Market movements are influenced by many factors – new data releases (economic or company-specific), geopolitical events, and sentiment. All are constantly updated in real time, with markets effectively constantly repricing for developments. This makes it difficult for individual investors to react efficiently to developments. However, might it be a futile endeavour to begin with?

THE EFFICIENT MARKET HYPOTHESIS

"How many efficient market theorists does it take to change a light bulb? None. If the light bulb needed changing the market would already have done it."[1] Eugene Fama's 1970 book *Efficient Capital Markets: A Review of Theory and Empirical Work* has fundamentally changed how we think about investing. Although not without controversy, his work eventually earned him a Nobel Prize in 2013, and every serious investor should understand its implications.

At its core, the "efficient market hypothesis" holds that "financial markets are effective in processing and reflecting all available

DOI: 10.4324/9781003792444-14

information … making it impossible for investors to consistently outperform the market based on information already known to the public." In simpler terms, the markets are so efficient that no one can gain a sustainable edge, and "actual prices at every point in time represent very good estimates of intrinsic values."[2]

Kahneman summarises this elegantly: "If all assets in a market are correctly priced, no one can expect to gain or lose by trading. Perfect prices leave no scope for cleverness."[3]

THE EMPIRICAL EVIDENCE

The theory has been debated and tested; and debated and tested again.

> Efficiency implies that simple trading rules ... should not work. This is a testable proposition, and an army of financial economists, including Gene [Fama], checked it. ... In any other field of human endeavour, seasoned professionals systematically outperform amateurs. But other fields are not so ruthlessly competitive as financial markets. ... Studies found, surprisingly, that the data are much closer to the efficient market prediction than anybody thought. Professional managers do not systematically outperform well-diversified passive investments.[4]

The empirical evidence supporting market efficiency is striking. Morningstar's long-term research found that over a ten-year period, the only actively managed funds that outperformed index funds even half the time were US small growth funds and emerging market funds. Other studies reveal that less than one in four of even the best-performing active fund managers consistently outperform index funds.[5]

A GREAT LEVELLER FOR INDIVIDUAL INVESTORS

If we accept Fama's theory, we're acknowledging that stocks trade at their fair value based on current information. This effectively eliminates the possibility of finding bargain shares overlooked by the market or selling "overvalued" shares before they decline. Even in its weakest form, the theory holds that all publicly available information is already "in the price."

The logical response? Hold equity exposures in index-tracking funds. There's little benefit to extensive financial analysis or paying higher fees to active fund managers. Technical analysis likewise offers limited value. Trying to identify under- or overvalued stocks becomes futile since all known information is reflected in market prices. The best way to achieve market returns is simply to own the entire market.

Future price movements become inherently "unpredictable" or follow a "random walk" independent of past movements. "For markets to continue falling or rising, more bad or good news is needed."[6]

The efficient market theory profoundly simplifies the stock market investing world. If market prices already reflect available information, the path to market-beating returns would come only through luck or taking greater risk – market-beating returns come from market-beating risk-taking. Stock prices constantly reprice as new information emerges, eliminating opportunities for risk-free profits through the actions of informed traders or algorithms.

As John Kay notes: "The good news is that the retail investor can take a free ride … you can be a beneficiary of the efficiency of financial markets."[7]

THE PARADOX OF EFFICIENT MARKETS

Tim Harford explains the paradox that the efficient market theory throws up in his book *The Undercover Economist*:

> the more rational the behaviour of ... investors the more erratic the behaviour of the stock-market becomes ... rational investors should be able to second-guess any predictable movements .... if it's predictable then, given the money at stake, they will predict it. But that means if investors really are rational ... all the predictability should be sucked out of the ... market.[8]
>
> ...because all trends will be anticipated. The only thing that is left is unpredictable news. [If this were true] that would be a paradox: perfectly formed investors produce a random market, but a random market doesn't reward anybody for becoming perfectly informed.[9]

CHALLENGE FROM BEHAVIOURAL ECONOMICS

If psychological biases impact investment decisions, as behavioural economics suggests, this could create market distortions that contradict efficient market theory – not just affecting individual investment behaviour, as we explored previously, but market pricing itself. Herding behaviour, recency bias, overconfidence, and loss aversion could all lead to inefficiencies that shouldn't exist in a truly efficient market.

The argument could be circular: if cognitive biases affect market efficiency, we are acknowledging they could affect our own investing too. In this case, behavioural discipline might matter more than sophisticated analysis. Humility is warranted – *if* professional market participants struggle to beat the market consistently, why should private investors expect to fare better? If any inefficiency exists, who is the most likely beneficiary? High-frequency algorithms account for significant trading volumes and quickly eliminate short-term inefficiencies. Similarly, professionals are also most likely to be the chief beneficiaries of any longer-term inefficiencies.

Perhaps the greatest concern for private investors isn't the theoretical debate between behavioural scientists and efficient market theorists, but how it's even possible to position a portfolio to benefit from any market inefficiencies that might exist.

THE IMPORTANCE OF ASSET ALLOCATION

A lot, if not most, private investors are highly focused on defining investing success on picking the right stocks and funds. "Stock picking as an investment philosophy … has gotten far too many retail investors burned in the process."[10] However, asset allocation, the strategic distribution of investments across different asset classes (for example, the proportion of equities across the entire portfolio), likely plays a far more significant role in determining long-term returns.

As we have seen, in the professional world, risk parameters are established at the board level and cascade downward through the organisation. Risk committees or risk management departments then articulate the risk tolerance defined at board level into a system of quantifiable limits and guidelines. The Risk Manager's role is crucial – transforming abstract risk tolerance concepts into clear, actionable frameworks that trading desks can readily implement and monitor.

Private investors adopting a similar approach could focus on recognising that asset allocation likely represents the most consequential investment decision that they need make. Individuals can establish their own hierarchy of investment choices, such as a minimum allocation to equities. How they then implement this practically (i.e. via which individual investments) can be found at the base of the hierarchy.

PRACTICAL CONSIDERATIONS: AN APPROACH FOR PRIVATE INVESTORS

Simple investing improvements include having a plan, the discipline to stick to it, and strict cost control to prevent fees from compounding over time. Diversification remains perhaps the closest thing to a "free lunch" in investing.

A practical approach for private investors might then look like this:

- Accept market efficiency: Acknowledge that the market is efficient enough that most investors – including professionals – find it difficult to beat consistently.
- Recognise technological realities: The chief beneficiaries of any inefficiencies that arise are likely to be institutions and professional investors, not private investors.
- Acknowledge behavioural limitations: Behavioural biases affect all investors to varying degrees, including ourselves.
- Build on solid foundations: Use market index funds as the foundation and ballast in your portfolio. Private investors may have little choice than to acknowledge that in the long run the best that can be hoped for is to achieve market returns, so a disciplined, low-cost, index-based approach will likely deliver the best long-term results.

This isn't necessarily bad – it cuts through much of the hassle associated with investing and leads to selecting instruments that will achieve market returns, like index funds.

CONCLUSION: FINDING CLARITY AMID THE NOISE

Amidst the often-contradictory information saturation that accompanies modern financial markets, efficient market hypothesis can offer a light by which to navigate. If markets are generally, or at least mostly, efficient, a sound strategy – perhaps the best one for most investors – is to embrace that efficiency rather than fight it.

By capturing market returns efficiently via the tools of asset allocation, cost control, and behavioural discipline, private investors can harness outcomes that ironically might exceed those trying to outsmart the market. This doesn't necessarily translate to abandoning active investment decisions altogether, but rather by focusing the core of a portfolio on low-cost index funds and accepting the limitations of our ability to beat the market consistently.

We live in a world of information overload. Market noise can be another source of it. There is wisdom in acknowledging what we don't know, embracing the market's efficiency, and positioning our portfolios accordingly.

NOTES

1 Paulos, John Allen *A Mathematician Plays the Market* (Penguin, 2003), page 160.
2 Logue, Ann C. "Are Markets Efficient? How Eugene Fama Kicked Off a Controversy" (*Britannica Money*, no date). https://www.britannica.com/money/what-is-the-efficient-market-hypothesis.
3 Kahneman, Daniel *Thinking, Fast and Slow* (Penguin, 2024), page 245.
4 Fama, Eugene F. "Efficient Markets, and the Nobel Prize" (University of Chicago Booth School of Business, no date). https://www.chicagobooth.edu/review/eugene-fama-efficient-markets-and-the-nobel-prize.
5 Corporate Finance Institute "Efficient Markets Hypothesis" (1 February 2018). https://corporatefinanceinstitute.com/resources/career-map/sell-side/capital-markets/efficient-markets-hypothesis/.
6 Lustig, Yoram *Saving and Investing for Retirement. The Definitive Handbook to Securing Your Financial Future* (Financial Times Guides, Pearson 2016), page 217.
7 Kay, John *The Long and the Short of It* (Profile Books, 2016), page 6.
8 Harford, Tim *The Undercover Economist* (Abacus, 2007), page 140.
9 Harford, Tim *The Undercover Economist* (Abacus, 2007), page 141.
10 Maggiulli, Nick *Just Keep Buying* (Harriman House, 2022), page 146.

REFERENCES

Corporate Finance Institute "Efficient Markets Hypothesis" (1 February 2018). https://corporatefinanceinstitute.com/resources/career-map/sell-side/capital-markets/efficient-markets-hypothesis/.

Fama, Eugene F. "Efficient Markets, and the Nobel Prize" (*University of Chicago Booth School of Business*, no date). https://www.chicagobooth.edu/review/eugene-fama-efficient-markets-and-the-nobel-prize.

Harford, Tim *The Undercover Economist* (Abacus, 2007).

Kahneman, Daniel *Thinking, Fast and Slow* (Penguin, 2024).

Kay, John *The Long and the Short of It* (Profile Books, 2016).

Logue, Ann C. "Are Markets Efficient? How Eugene Fama Kicked Off a Controversy" (*Britannica Money*, no date). https://www.britannica.com/money/what-is-the-efficient-market-hypothesis.

Lustig, Yoram *Saving and Investing for Retirement. The Definitive Handbook to Securing Your Financial Future* (Financial Times Guides, Pearson, 2016).

Maggiulli, Nick *Just Keep Buying* (Harriman House, 2022).

Paulos, John Allen *A Mathematician Plays the Market* (Penguin, 2003).

15

THE PRICE OF SUPERIOR LONG-TERM GAINS

Stock markets have historically risen spectacularly over the long term. However, markets are inherently volatile. This rise has not by any means been linear. Periodic drawdowns (where the market falls from a record high) are not just possible but an expected feature of investing. "On average, the market declines by about 13.7% at some point within a given year."[1] Accepting this volatility is the price of admittance, if you will, to the club of higher long-term returns.

It is guaranteed at some point during your investment journey you will face the harsh reality of losing money. That loss is likely to be substantial at some point. I mention this not to scare you away – quite the opposite. By preparing yourself mentally, you'll know what to do and perhaps most importantly, what *not* to do when these inevitable downturns occur.

PREPARING FOR THE INEVITABLE

A few years ago, I read an article that changed how I fly. People die in otherwise survivable crashes because they freeze. This happens because in the traumatic aftermath of a crash, you're faced with a scenario you've tried to deny could ever happen to you. You may have seen the safety demonstration hundreds of times, but in the immediate shock and confusion, it becomes difficult to think clearly and carry out evacuation procedures safely.

What I try to do now is visualise the safety briefing to internalise the information. I check that my life vest is where it should be and count the number of rows to the nearest exit (which may be

DOI: 10.4324/9781003792444-15

behind me) in case it's dark or smoky and I need to know which way to go. Mentally rehearsing different scenarios, I hope, will maximise my chances of survival should the unthinkable happen.

In investing, the chance of facing a downturn or crash isn't remote – it's guaranteed if you invest for long enough. Unlike an actual plane crash, freezing and doing nothing during a market crash might actually be the best response. Nonetheless, it's worth considering these scenarios ahead of time.

In times of market volatility, keep this chapter close. Re-read it before deciding how to react. It may save you not just a lot of worry but benefit you by keeping your focus on your long-term goals.

UNDERSTANDING MARKET CYCLES

By looking at history, we can examine what has happened before and use this information to construct expectations about what comes next. Market crashes can differ significantly from one another, making each feel unprecedented. The newspapers will likely tell you it's unprecedented, but remember that their business is selling news. Yet even when the immediate context of a current crash seems remarkably different, market crashes, reduced to their core elements, often follow strikingly familiar patterns.

While crashes are often sudden, they're typically triggered by the interplay of various factors – economic, financial, psychological, or external:

- Financial imbalances: Excessive leverage, asset bubbles, or risk premiums reduced to levels that leave no margin for anything less than the most optimistic outcomes create precarious conditions. When investors are highly leveraged, even small market movements can trigger forced selling, amplifying downturns.
- Political events: Growing international tensions, wars (trade or outright), or unexpected policy changes introduce uncertainty that markets typically abhor. The announcement of new tariffs, geopolitical conflicts, or radical policy shifts can send markets into tailspins as investors reassess risk.

- Economic shocks: Recessions, sudden rises in interest rates, or banking crises can dramatically alter market sentiment overnight. When central banks unexpectedly raise rates or economic data reveals a contraction, markets often respond with immediate selling pressure.

The transition from bull to bear market may be accompanied by high-market valuations where equities have become overvalued relative to historical averages, or a slowdown in earnings growth. Interest rates may be rising to tame inflation, with higher borrowing costs leading to slower economic growth. As prices fall, the decline can develop its own momentum as traders look for support levels that ultimately fail.

From a psychological perspective, investor sentiment evolves from optimism to euphoria during the latter stages of a bull market, and as it transitions to a bear market growing anxiety may eventually give way to sheer panic. Cognitive biases – overconfidence during bull markets, loss aversion in bear markets – will have a significant influence over market dynamics.

These psychological factors then create their own momentum. Herd behaviour can transform a loss of market confidence into outright panic selling. Michael Sincere notes in *Predict the Next Bull or Bear Market and Win*: "Retail investors have an established pattern of selling all their stocks near the bottom"[2] – and for good reason: "at the beginning of a bull market, few investors believe it has started. At the end of a bull market, few accept that it's ending … no market goes straight up or down."[3]

We can conceptualise this as a cycle with distinct phases that tend to repeat throughout market history:

1 Early bull market: Prices will be depressed, and pessimism will be extremely high. Nonetheless, the market eventually finds a bottom and prices begin to increase. It is rare for investors to recognise this phase while it's happening – as most will be nursing scarring recent losses and be wary of so-called "dead cat bounces." Often the greatest opportunities can be found at this point in the cycle, but it is mostly market contrarians or those with a strong conviction who benefit from these.

2 Growing bull market: As the market rises, participation broadens as more investors grow in confidence. Economic indicators may improve, and media coverage turns positive. Corporate earnings typically strengthen during this phase, providing fundamental support for higher prices. Professional institutional investors increase equity allocations and retail investors, previously cautious, will start to reappear on the market.
3 Maturing bull market: The markets then will likely exhaust a bull market by entering a period of excess with widespread euphoria. Market prices become increasingly stretched, speculative behaviour becomes rampant, and explanations of "why this time is different" become commonplace. Investors disregard valuation metrics at historic extremes with justifications, such as of structural realignment, that create a narrative reinforcing the prevailing market level.
4 Market peak: The peak will likely be reached by regular all-time market highs and choppy price action leading into a decline. Before the peak itself, market breadth begins to contract, with fewer stocks contributing to the gains and some technical indicators may start showing warning signs that are usually more obvious only in retrospect.
5 Bear market: The decline phase can be prolonged and is likely accompanied by a deterioration in economic indicators and poorer corporate earnings. At the start of a bear market, there may be a "buy the dip" attitude still quite prevalent among market participants, but each rally fails to reach previous highs. The media will turn increasingly negative and market sentiment becomes increasingly fearful.
6 Market bottom: As the market reaches its low point, sentiment becomes extremely negative, prices very low, and all-round loss of confidence is prevalent across the market. Valuation metrics can reach historically attractive levels, but amidst widespread pessimism few investors have courage or capital to exploit the current pricing levels.
7 The cycle repeats: However, it is never in exactly the same way or to the same timeline.

Tempting as it may be to try and identify the exact peak of bull market euphoria or depth of bear market pessimism, in practice this is extraordinarily difficult. "No one can consistently predict what the market will do tomorrow, next week or next year … many people try."[4] Getting it wrong means missing out on upside as markets continue to march higher, buying in too early in a bear market and watching your investments fall anyway, or buying back too late having missed much of the recovery.

Several factors make market timing challenging:

- Each market cycle has multiple elements to it that are unique. Studying historical comparisons may not be a reliable way to predict what happens next. The tech bubble of the late 1990s, the financial crisis of 2008, and the pandemic crash of 2020 all had different causes, trajectories, and recovery patterns.
- Frequently, the peak of euphoria or depth of pessimism is only obvious in the rearview mirror. While living through either, the prevailing narratives can be convincing enough to cloud judgement. It can be difficult to think one step back from the rest of the herd as opposed to knowing when it is appropriate to take a contrarian viewpoint.
- External shocks can cause a sudden shift in market dynamics that no one can reasonably predict. These are perhaps more likely to be sharp and on the negative side.
- Market watchers must cut through noise and short-term factors that may no longer reflect longer-term trends. Daily price movements sometimes reflect only technical factors or liquidity issues.
- Volatility may obscure underlying factors and trends, or make it nigh on impossible to distinguish between temporary movements and the start of a new phase.
- Counter-movements can appear convincing. False signals are common, and when genuine movements do occur, they can be swift and be well underway before trend confirmation.
- Overconfidence, or loss aversion, can further distort perceptions and decision-making ability.

Trying to trade your way through these cycles – in other words, timing the market – is therefore unlikely to work for a lot of investors. If you were able to successfully time the market, you would already be out by the time the market saw very large falls.

Once they start to occur, you would be under a lot of psychological pressure and emotion. If you were worried and potentially losing sleep over what was happening, you *would be* making any subsequent decisions from a position of fear. To put it mildly, this isn't the best time to make rational decisions about long-term asset allocation and investing strategy. The blend of transaction costs, tax implications, and the high probability of mistiming the market can very easily lead to portfolio underperformance compared to a disciplined, long-term approach.

PSYCHOLOGICAL RESPONSES

If seeing the market down is going to be shocking, the idea of regular market cycles – although difficult to predict in advance – should nonetheless provide some comfort. Understanding that the market works this way underlines that there will be a time when you will lose money, and likely lose a lot, but it won't be permanent, at least if history is anything to go by. In retrospect, historic periods can seem less scary than the present day, but that is because we know in the past recovery followed crash, and this time we are only hoping that that stays true. The gap between intellectual understanding and emotional reality can be vast when real money is at stake and vaster still if that real money represents your financial independence pot.

Stock markets go up, as well as spectacularly down, at times; but over time they have still managed to deliver outstanding returns – and because they rise over time frequently hit all-time highs, but an ultimate peak is never truly reached.

We may rationally accept that markets ebb and flow. But in a "down" situation where we can measure losses in cold hard cash terms, and the mere act of logging into our investment account comes with an accompanying sinking feeling ("how much money have I lost today"), it is very easy for even the most sensible and level-headed of investors to do something impulsive that they will later come to regret.

Many investors may overestimate their resilience in the face of actual financial losses. "Minimizing possible regret often plays too large a role in investors' decision-making."[5] Rational consumer behaviour completely reverses when it comes to financial markets.

> When the supermarket has a sale, say on toilet paper, the consumer runs in and stocks up. But when the housing or stock market has a sale, most often called a crash or correction, the same consumer often runs away from it. When the supermarket raises its prices, the consumer shops somewhere else. But when housing or the stock market raise their prices, the same consumer often rushes in and starts buying.[6]

THE CHALLENGE OF MARKET SENTIMENT

There is no challenge in being optimistic in a bull market (a period when prices are going up over a sustained period of time). In fact, it is quite easy. The general sentiment across the market is one of optimism, with positive expectations for future returns. Although bull markets can last for years, they inevitably, eventually end.

It is far harder to remain optimistic about meeting your long-term financial goals when market sentiment turns. The imbalance thrown up by loss aversion may lead to investors selling whole portfolios in a panic, crystallising losses instead of staying the course and waiting for prices to recover.

Acknowledging loss aversion is one thing we can do to make us more resilient investors. But it is easier said than done. Your rational self may know full well that prices have always gone on to newer highs, even after the most violent selloffs. But in the middle of a pullback, it is all too easy to lose sight of this.

If your investment pot is your largest asset, how are you going to feel if you are losing money that you have worked hard to accumulate through diligent budget-keeping and squirreling away savings each month? When the amount that your portfolio is down by has taken years to accumulate?

The psychological impact of losses becomes more severe as portfolio values increase. Consider the following example:

- £250,000 portfolio: 30% decline = £75,000 loss
- £500,000 portfolio: 30% decline = £150,000 loss
- £1,000,000 Portfolio: 30% decline = £300,000 loss

When you are in it, you will almost certainly want to change tack and do something, and that something is highly likely to be to quit. If you quit, you won't be back for a long, long time.

Ken Fisher, writing in the *Daily Telegraph*, says:

> For four decades, I've dubbed the stock market "the Great Humiliator". It craves tricking everyone as badly as possible, for as long as possible, for as much money as possible ... it operates by luring investors slowly as stocks climb higher. Then a bear market starts gently, pickpocketing investors via dips cast as buying opportunities, pulling in more money. Finally, late, near the bottom, it hammers them with near vertical declines, terrifying and making them feel like fools. Most then rush to cash out – only to get whipsawed as the next bull market lifts off. Then the cycle begins again.[7]

Far from trying to put us off, this serves as a stark warning about the dangers of trying to time the market for the unwary:

> Consider the wisdom of Charlie Munger, Warren Buffett's long-term business partner: "If you're not willing to react with equanimity to a market price decline of 50% two or three times a century ... you deserve the mediocre result you are going to get".[8]

PRACTICAL STRATEGIES FOR PSYCHOLOGICAL RESILIENCE

The most successful investors aren't those who never feel fear or anxiety about market declines – they're those who have systems in place that allow them to continue investing despite these feelings.

1. PREPARATION BEFORE MARKET DOWNTURNS

- Accept that market volatility is part and parcel of stock market investing.
- The price of admittance to higher returns is that those returns are not linear. Any downsides are included in the average return.
- Consider your investment strategy when you can do so with a "cold" head and create written investment principles and limits (e.g. regarding asset allocation) that you can refer to during emotional moments.

- Consider how you can stick with your plan – ahead of time – and remove the opportunity to make emotive decisions in the heat of market volatility.

2. DURING MARKET DOWNTURNS

- Remember that you have history on your side: no matter how big declines have been, markets have always recovered and gone on to make higher highs.
- Any hit to your portfolio will therefore be temporary. Temporary declines are a feature of the market and normal. Markets mean-revert (return towards average returns over the long term). If you are experiencing poor returns, a period is likely to follow where you have outsized returns in relation to systematic market returns.
- Maintain focus on your long-term financial plan rather than short-term volatility.
- The pain of watching the value of your investment decline is real. The temptation to do something, anything, to stem the losses are natural human responses.
- If necessary, delete any investment apps but certainly avoid checking portfolio values daily.
- Consider market declines as opportunities to buy investments "on sale."
- Above all, remember: "if you go through life worried about the next stock market crash or correction, it's likely you will miss out on many profitable opportunities."[9]

Market cyclicality is an immutable law of investing. Recoveries often follow crashes, frequently in quick succession. Even the most severe market downturns represent part of the investment journey. The disciplined investor who adheres to their strategy not only weathers these storms but emerges stronger when markets (inevitably) recover.

NOTES

1 Maggiulli, Nick *Just Keep Buying* (Harriman House, 2022), page 193.
2 Sincere, Michael *Predict the Next Bull or Bear Market and Win* (Sincere Books, 2014), page 119.

3 Sincere, Michael *Predict the Next Bull or Bear Market and Win* (Sincere Books, 2014), page 68.
4 Sincere, Michael *Predict the Next Bull or Bear Market and Win* (Sincere Books, 2014), page 10.
5 Paulos, John Allen *A Mathematician Plays the Market* (Penguin, 2003), page 23.
6 Kiyosaki, Robert T. *Rich Dad, Poor Dad* (Plata Publishing, 2011), pages 231–232.
7 Fisher, Ken "Don't Be Fooled into Thinking a Bear Market Has Begun" (*The Telegraph*, 19 August 2024). https://www.telegraph.co.uk/money/investing/dont-let-stocks-plunge-fool-you-bear-market-begun/.
8 Maggiulli, Nick *Just Keep Buying* (Harriman House, 2022), page 201.
9 Sincere, Michael *Predict the Next Bull or Bear Market and Win* (Sincere Books, 2014), page 67.

REFERENCES

Fisher, Ken "Don't Be Fooled into Thinking a Bear Market Has Begun" (*The Telegraph*, 19 August 2024). https://www.telegraph.co.uk/money/investing/dont-let-stocks-plunge-fool-you-bear-market-begun/.

Kiyosaki, Robert T. *Rich Dad, Poor Dad* (Plata Publishing, 2011).

Maggiulli, Nick *Just Keep Buying* (Harriman House, 2022).

Paulos, John Allen *A Mathematician Plays the Market* (Penguin, 2003).

Sincere, Michael *Predict the Next Bull or Bear Market and Win* (Sincere Books, 2014).

16

INVESTING SYSTEMATICALLY

POUND-COST AVERAGING

When Joe called me in a state of near panic, I knew the currency markets had gotten to him again.

Joe was in the process of moving back to England after years of living and working in Europe. He had built up quite a nice nest egg and was planning to use it to buy a property. His deposit was in euros (EUR), but the property he wanted was in Central London – so he would be paying for it in pounds (GBP).

He was keen to minimise the mortgage he would have to raise, making up the difference between the price he had agreed to pay and how much his deposit would end up being, once converted to pounds.

Naturally, Joe wanted to maximise the EUR/GBP exchange rate he achieved to receive as many pounds as he could for his euros. (Joe had already set up a dedicated account with an online money transfer service. He could fix the foreign exchange rate when the market "was good enough," avoiding bank transfers where he would have less control over the rate, and where he would probably pay more in fees and charges.)

Joe had a window of two months until he needed his deposit to be in pounds and was keen to obtain the best possible exchange rate in that timeframe.

THE GREED AND FEAR EMOTIONAL CYCLE

Joe began constantly checking what the market was doing, searching for every possible bit of news, forecast, or analyst commentary he could find. It became more than his latest hobby and certainly not one he was enjoying in the slightest.

DOI: 10.4324/9781003792444-16

In my dealing roles, I would spend a decent proportion of my time looking across multiple market screens of flickering price quotes, news, and charts slicing data into every possible array a dealer could need. But in this case, there was little need for such complexity. I could tell if EUR/GBP was rising, or falling, simply by Joe's anxiety levels.

When the price dipped a little, he'd go into full panic mode. But when the market rose a little, he suddenly felt emboldened that he had been right all along for waiting – which meant he would promptly hold off doing anything again. "It's going higher still," he would surmise, the pain of the slight dip immediately forgotten.

The "greed and fear" cycle that drives financial markets was playing out in his personal transaction. The cycle would repeat, but each time he was falling into the trap of "anchoring" his expectations at the best previous high point he could have achieved, almost as if the market now "owed" him at least that level.

"I have lost £1,000 today!" Joe announced one morning. "I had a feeling I should have exchanged my deposit at market open. What should I do?" he asked me. (Well, what he actually said was, "You work with FX, what would you do?" What he was really inviting was where did I think the peak FX rate was in the next two months?)

If I knew the answer to that, this would be a very different type of book. As he was after my professional opinion, I answered by highlighting the way most companies that I have worked for would answer the question.

CORPORATE FX RISK MANAGEMENT

Companies would view Joe's exposure as a financial risk to manage, in accordance with their Treasury policy. Their principal concern would be that exchange rates moved against them, causing a financial loss and possibly risking the ability to proceed with the purchase or only being able to do so at additional cost.

Imagine a UK company expecting €1 million in revenue next quarter but needing to pay £800,000 in costs. A 10% drop in EUR/GBP could eliminate their profit margin entirely. The most common objective in such circumstances would be to minimise the risk of this volatility and protect the economics of the transaction.

We have no idea about the future outcome of the exchange rate, and there's a chance it could be higher or lower. In that case, one outcome is that it would have been better to have sold the currency at the start, and the other is that it would have been better to do nothing and take the future rate at the point of execution.

A logical response, therefore, given what could be viewed as a heads-or-tails outcome, is to manage half of the exposure by selling half of the currency now and the other half when needed right before exchange.

That is one reason why companies may manage (or "hedge") only part of their exposure.[1]

When deciding to buy the property, Joe would have had a budget in mind. He had an idea about how much his EUR deposit would be worth against the asking price, within his budget. Let's assume Joe was happy with this base case by choosing to put in an offer and proceed with the purchase once it was accepted.

For companies, managing financial risks is something that investors would think is within the competency of management to control, or at least minimise to the extent that is possible. This is partly because most companies with significant FX exposures in their business model are likely to pursue some form of risk mitigation and hedging. Such being the case, investors may expect their peers to do so as well. This creates a feedback loop where there is now an expectation that this is within management control and should be done.

There are reasons not to manage exposures. One might be if the company can pass on the impact of FX movements to customers (but Joe was unlikely to agree with the seller that if EUR fell in value against GBP, he should get a discount off the agreed price, particularly as he could lock in the rate by not waiting to exchange his euros).

If Joe's property purchase was being managed along corporate lines, therefore, chances are part of the exposure (probably at least 50%) would simply be sold mechanically at the point the offer was accepted. Exchanging the rest now would mean Joe would know with certainty how much he would get. If the amount he could receive today meant he could still comfortably complete his purchase, many in Joe's position might simply ignore the opportunity cost and do exactly that.

The cost of "hedging the exposure" in this manner is that you actively give up the possibility to benefit from favourable movements in market rates. However, in exchange you get certainty. In Joe's case, this meant he could fix the amount he needed to borrow.

INTRODUCING POUND-COST AVERAGING

But Joe wasn't a multinational corporation with a Treasury department. He needed a solution that was both practical and psychologically manageable. I could see Joe viewed this corporate approach as a cop-out.

"Well, for companies there is little to be gained even if their Treasury departments had a strong conviction on the future direction of rates," I conceded. This is true – it basically translates as taking an active decision not to manage a risk. Most Treasury policies I have seen have a clause against active speculation, which is exactly what Joe was essentially doing.

A sizeable FX profit would be viewed by management as resulting from unhedged risk that happened to go in their favour, at least this time, but might not at other times. "We are in the business of making toilet brushes, not speculating on the financial markets," a Finance Director might retort.[2]

Instead, I asked Joe, "What would a good outcome look like for you?"

He paused. I let him think.

"Well, I really don't want to miss out on the chance of getting better gains … but I'm worried the market may fall as well," Joe finally said. "I know I'm unlikely to get the very best rate," he admitted, "but I don't want to get the worst one either. It's a lot of money!"

If we accept that markets are efficient (and FX is a deep 24-hour market), everything known about the exchange rate is factored into the current price. News is constant, and the market is therefore constantly being repriced. If Joe waits with any portion of his conversion, the outcome is better, worse, or the same, depending on whether the market moves in his favour, against him, or doesn't do very much at all.

It made sense to switch at least a portion. The rest needed a technique that would allow some participation in any beneficial market movements while not losing the ability to sleep at night.

"What if you could get nearer the average of the two?" I asked.

"I'd be happy with that, I think" he said. "But how can I do that?"

"What if you exchange the amount you're comfortable with today – that could be the 50% we talked about – and then equal chunks on set days, spaced equally?" I suggested. "Or, if you prefer, you could just divide your total euro amount by ten, one for this week and nine for the next nine weeks and do it that way."

"You mean exchange some today, Tuesday, and then a tenth of the balance next Tuesday and so on every week until I've converted all my euros?" Joe asked.

"Exactly. That way you're selling your euros at regular intervals and averaging out the achieved rate throughout the two-month period. This technique will reduce your timing risk and help you avoid the danger of converting all your euros at what, in hindsight, turns out to be an inopportune moment."

"… and I have a plan about when and how I'm going to convert my euros!"

"Yes, Joe, and you have a plan about when and how you're going to convert your euros!"

The change was immediate and visible. Joe's shoulders fell, and a smile spread over his face as he reached for his coffee. I could see the stress of trying to time the market lift. The technique I had told him about, called "pound-cost averaging," meant that since all conversions would be made at varying price points, he was no longer at risk of exchanging a large amount at an outlying and unfavourable time.

This greatly simplified his strategy and likely mitigated a pending sudden emotional decision based on an abrupt decline. Joe went from checking exchange rates obsessively every hour to calmly executing his predetermined plan. He had traded the anxiety of perfect timing for the peace of mind that comes with systematic execution.

He did reasonably well and (more or less) stuck to the discipline of following the plan. Most importantly, he was able to worry about other aspects of the property purchase rather than how he was going to convert his euros. And he always buys me a pint whenever I see him.

USING POUND-COST AVERAGING FOR INVESTING

There are solid differences between currency markets, where the value of one currency is weighed against another, and stock markets, which over time tend to rise. However, in the very short term, both are volatile places where prices ebb and flow, and concerns about market timing can be broadly similar. Understanding how to navigate these timing concerns is crucial for building a successful long-term investment strategy, regardless of the specific market you're investing in.

Pound-cost averaging isn't a complex investment strategy. All it requires is investing a fixed amount regularly (such as monthly). It works particularly well with regular investments, such as immediately after payday, via direct debit, or from pension contributions made via salary sacrifice. Many providers enable auto-invest, which means your contributions will be invested according to predetermined investment allocations you've set up, or default ones in company pension schemes.

REMOVING EMOTIONAL DECISION-MAKING: THE DISCIPLINE ADVANTAGE

The biggest advantage of pound-cost averaging is that it provides a long-term approach that can reduce the emotional impact of constantly making short-term decisions as to what and when to buy after each payday. This can really come into its own during times of market volatility where maintaining long-term perspective can come under challenge.

Once you've set up the system, it requires minimal maintenance. You won't need to constantly monitor the market and feel the need to react to news items.

Over time, your purchase price is averaged out, and so the impact of where in the market cycle (near highs or lows) your purchases occur is reduced, and the risk of a particular price point being an outlier is mitigated.

THE MECHANICS OF PRICE AVERAGING

However, pound-cost averaging not only smooths the achieved prices, but can lead to better actual financial outcomes. When prices are high, you buy fewer units, but when prices are lower, you benefit from buying more units. There is an immediate comfort during short-term price falls knowing that you will end up buying more units than if prices were always relentlessly marching higher. However, as pound-cost averaging ends up not only "averaging" the price, but does so on a weighted basis, this means that you end up with potentially better outcomes financially as well.

EXAMPLE

Consider Martin, who invests £500 monthly.

In January, shares cost 100p each (resulting in 500 shares).

In February, they drop to 80p (meaning Martin buys 625 shares).

By March, they rise to 120p (resulting in 417 shares).

The average cost per unit can be calculated by dividing the total amount invested by the number of units purchased. In Martin's cases, his average cost is 96p per share—better than the 100p average market price over those three months.

WHY POUND-COST AVERAGING BEATS BUY THE DIP

Pound-cost averaging can also beat market timing – even if you knew *exactly* when the market was at the absolute lowest point in between two all-time highs (and kept new funds in cash until this time). In other words, if you had *perfect* knowledge and so could always buy at the lowest possible price – you would still underperform pound-cost averaging – and do so 70% of the time. This is because dips simply do not happen often enough and the market keeps rising in between, meaning that staying in cash means you miss out on compounding.[3]

WHEN POUND-COST AVERAGING WORKS BEST

Pound-cost averaging works naturally when the amounts you're seeking to invest come to you over time, such as in each month's pay packet.

When you have a large amount to deploy in one go (such as from an annual bonus payment or inheritance), it will probably serve you better to deploy larger sums in lump-sum form rather than spread over time. The money has longer to compound if put to work at once, and if the market rises (as stock markets tend to) your entire sum benefits immediately. Lump-sum investment puts your funds to work straight away. In a steadily rising market, getting in at the earliest point can lead to the most profitable outcome.

THE PSYCHOLOGICAL FACTOR

However, market timing risk remains real. For investors who are more cautious and wish to spread risk, pound-cost averaging even a large lump sum and drip-feeding it into the market may help them sleep better – and that's reason alone. The potential disappointment and regret from a market correction right after a lump-sum investment needs to be weighed against the higher average acquisition cost from pursuing pound-cost averaging in a steadily rising market.

This might seem counterintuitive, but falling prices can in fact be your friend. Every month, you're buying more shares at lower prices. Pound-cost averaging will average the purchase price downward, but you may stay investing when everything else is telling you to steer clear. In hindsight, you may be very glad that you did. You only need the market to recover before you start withdrawing funds – potentially decades away.

From this perspective, once you've made your investments and are following a passive strategy, it doesn't actually matter how much your portfolio is worth at any given point during the accumulation phase. What you should care about is how much it will be worth when you come to access the funds.

When you're making an actual investment (your monthly contribution), and prices are down, you're getting more units for your money – and you want to buy each unit at the lowest price possible. This will be easier the earlier you are in your investing journey. Not only is there a long-time horizon for your portfolio to recover, but you'll have more money left to invest in your future investment journey than you'll have invested up to that point. It makes sense to want to invest each of these pounds at the lowest possible price.

NOTES

1 A complication for companies is that given the complexity of businesses and possibly a myriad of currency flows, the exact future currency requirement may need to be forecasted based on a series of assumptions, so that there will be some degree of uncertainty, and that is another, not inconsequential, reason why the whole forecasted exposure may not be hedged. But let's put those aside for the sake of the current example.

2 Granted, FX exposures can be huge: one company I worked for could be impacted by about USD 1 billion for each 10 cents of movement in EUR/USD rates if they did nothing to manage their FX risk. Ignoring the sums involved, another way to look at it was that if there were a 5% profit margin on a deal, and there was a complete mismatch between the currencies of revenue and cost, a 5% FX movement in the exchange rate would wipe out profitability. This is of greater concern than, say, ending up with a 6% or 7% profit margin by calling the market right.

3 Analysis by Maggiulli, Nick "Even God Couldn't Beat Dollar-Cost Averaging" (*Of Dollars and Data*, 5 February 2019) (accessed 6 March 2026). https://ofdollarsanddata.com/even-god-couldnt-beat-dollar-cost-averaging/.

REFERENCE

Maggiulli, Nick "Even God Couldn't Beat Dollar-Cost Averaging" (*Of Dollars and Data*, 5 February 2019) (accessed 6 March 2026). https://ofdollarsanddata.com/even-god-couldnt-beat-dollar-cost-averaging/.

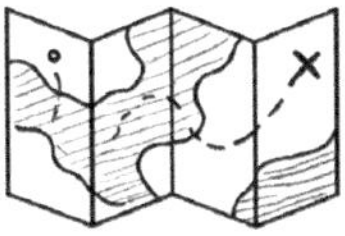

17

WHAT YOU CONTROL

As Covid-19 reminded us, markets and global events are always unpredictable. At times, it can seem that factors beyond our control can significantly impact our financial trajectory, but it's important to remember there are a large number of variables that are entirely within your control.

This chapter focuses on those variables. These can truly make the difference between your financial success and falling short of your goals.

A good place to start is recapping some of the rules from earlier in this book.

STAYING DISCIPLINED WITH REGULAR CONTRIBUTIONS

The discipline to maintain regular, consistent contributions (regardless of what is happening in the markets) sounds simple, but sticking with it over the long term is powerful. There is a reason why this factor is first on the list.

It is very easy to let the feeling that you are throwing good money after bad during market downturns override the plan that you have formulated. It is precisely during such times, when the market is on sale, that historically the best long-term gains have been planted. As markets recover, disciplined investors have been rewarded with outstanding returns.

THE POWER OF STARTING EARLY

Time amplifies each pound you invest, as we have seen. As Robert Stone notes: "[T]he main principle with all pension provision is

DOI: 10.4324/9781003792444-17

that the sooner you start saving money in a pension plan the more you will have at retirement."[1]

SAVINGS RATIO VERSUS RETURN

Your savings rate often has a more dramatic impact on your financial independence timeline than chasing an extra percentage point of return. Many people home in on investment returns, but even if you are able to achieve alpha this can be difficult to maintain – unlike your savings rate, which is entirely within your influence.

The lifestyle that you choose to lead is the direct inverse of this and another thing well within your control. Stay on top of lifestyle creep, and beware – it can be hard to go back. For example, if you decide from now on that you'll only take business class flights, it may be difficult to start flying with budget airlines or even economy class again.

LIFESTYLE CHOICES: THE DIDEROT EFFECT

"Regrets on Parting with My Old Dressing Gown" is an essay by the eighteenth-century French philosopher Denis Diderot in which he highlighted a social phenomenon that today still bears his name: the "Diderot effect."[2]

The essay concerns how receiving the gift of a luxurious dressing gown, which stood out among his other possessions, triggered a cascade of additional purchases to complement the original gift. This behaviour in psychology can be driven by the desire to maintain equilibrium in lifestyle and can lead to a chain reaction unleashing further consumption. In Diderot's case, it resulted in transforming his simple (and comfortable) life into one of financial strain.

Now imagine you really did decide to start flying business class. Granted, it comes with some perks, such as lounge access (usually) and perhaps fast track through security. But if your experience at the airport really is enhanced, what else might you want? Maybe you wouldn't be content with taking the coach to the airport, opting for a taxi instead. You might also extend this to your destination and choose to stay in a more luxurious hotel. To align with the elevated status of flying business class, you may spend more on travel accessories, high-end luggage, premium noise-cancelling headphones, stylish attire, or upgrade to the latest gadgets, tablets, e-readers, or laptops for in-flight entertainment.

STRATEGIES TO COMBAT LIFESTYLE INFLATION

A clear budget will help prevent overspending. Be intentional with your purchases. Reflect on why you want to buy something new and consider the long-term implications of acquiring it. Is it a need or a want? Be aware of whether you may be starting an upgrade cycle. For some people, holding off on a purchase, if undecided, and implementing a "waiting period" might be helpful. Delaying gratification can help eliminate impulse buying.

Also, be aware of any social pressures that may be driving you to make additional purchases. Advertising, trends, and simple peer pressure can all contribute to the Diderot effect.

Decluttering can help you identify items you no longer need, but the frequent practice itself can help shift your focus from acquiring material possessions toward appreciating what you already have. Practising gratitude, and contentment, not only diminishes the drive to continually acquire new items to enhance your lifestyle but can shift your outlook to valuing experiences over material possessions. Not only can that help you lead a more fulfilled life, but you'll notice the difference in your pocket too.

REVISITING YOUR FINANCIAL PLAN PERIODICALLY

During your portfolio's accumulation phase, it makes sense to revisit your financial independence number annually. You may decide that you can afford a better lifestyle because of the size of your pot. If so, great; that can be a reward for your hard work to date. Equally, your plan may have gotten off track. Being aware of this can allow you to make any necessary adjustments.

HEALTH: YOUR MOST IMPORTANT ASSET

Being ready to retire while you still have enough health to enjoy the fruits of your career and years of having worked, saved, and invested is crucial. Most individuals prepare for retirement by trying to optimise their investments and save enough. However, investing in your health should also not be neglected. Health is the basic building block of everything.

The healthier you are, the more you can earn (if you need to) and the more time you have to enjoy what you've saved. Exercise and eat well – there's no point saving all that money if you're not around to enjoy it. One of the biggest things that can influence mental health is having a purpose in life.

STAY ON TOP OF FEES AND COSTS

Investment costs and management fees can act as a silent wealth eroder. We have considered the power of compounding when it comes to investment returns. Fees and costs compound in the same way but work against the portfolio's growth. Costs can sound small, but the mathematics over the long term can be unforgiving.

Management fees may not be heavily scrutinised by investors, but they should be. If you pay 1% in management fees and make a return of 6%, your portfolio only grows by 5%. A £100,000 portfolio (without any further contributions) achieving a 5% average annual growth rate will be worth £432,000 after 30 years. The same portfolio achieving the full 6% will grow to £574,000. The total portfolio will be worth almost a third more if the fees could have been eliminated.

Platform fees, bid-ask spreads, performance fees, dealing costs, account fees, and the like should all be carefully researched, monitored, and managed. There are some very low-cost options available, and the compounding effect on your returns can be staggering over an investment lifetime.

TAX EFFICIENCY

Another thing that is definitely in your control is whether or not you hold your investments in a tax-efficient manner. In the UK, you can do this by making use of your annual pension and ISA contribution allowances.

Pensions may seem "mundane," but let's reframe that perception. What we're really talking about here is a tax wrapper around your investment portfolio – one of the most efficient ones currently available in the UK. Along with Individual Savings Accounts (ISAs), they are tools that should form part of your plan.

The key difference between ISAs and pensions is the tax point. For ISAs, it's at the outset. Any contributions come from your post-tax net pay. Once within the wrapper, your investments can grow free of further tax, and there's no tax to pay when withdrawals are made.

Pension contributions are generally made from your pre-tax pay, if made via salary sacrifice, or with the tax claimed back subsequently, thereby essentially from your gross pay. Once inside the wrapper, your investments again grow free from capital gains and other taxes, but when you withdraw an amount, this is added to your income for that tax year.

A key determinant of whether to prioritise ISAs or pensions, at a high-level, is your expected tax rate in the year of contribution versus the tax rate in the tax year when you expect to withdraw the funds. If you are a higher rate taxpayer now, but expect to be a basic rate payer later, it can make sense to focus on contributing to your pension first. In the UK, 25% of pension cash withdrawals are currently tax-free up to a £268,275 limit. So, if you expect to remain a basic rate taxpayer there are still likely to be tax advantages in prioritising pension contributions, up to your ability to fully take advantage of this allowance.

If you did expect your effective tax rate to be identical, whether you need flexibility to access your funds earlier is likely to be the determining factor.[3] Alternatively, if you expect to have a higher income tax rate after retirement, ISAs might be the more attractive option now. Making use of employer pension contribution matching is likely to be worth it in any case, as otherwise you'd be saying no to "free money."

STRATEGIC WITHDRAWAL PLANNING

You can use ISAs and private pensions in combination to withdraw from your pot in the most tax-efficient way possible. Naturally, this will impact the longevity of your pot, so it's important to look for the optimal combination.

When planning for this, or FIRE (Financial Independence, Retire Early), do take account of the fact that the portion of your pot within pensions might not be available yet – at the point you transition away from your main career or until you reach a certain qualifying age. Part-time income, passive income, and drawings from ISAs or GIA (General Investment Accounts – unwrapped trading accounts), premium bonds, and the like will need to bridge the gap until you can access your pension funds.

The tax advantages that pensions offer are too good to ignore. The current UK pension freedoms have made them into a flexible and key component of your financial independence planning. When considering drawdown sequence, pensions are suitable for access later in life. No plan is complete without their inclusion. (Likewise, the state pension should form part of your planning.)

REBALANCING

Periodic rebalancing (adjusting the investment mix in your portfolio) is necessary to maintain your target asset allocation. As markets rise, your equity allocation may well rise above the target percentage, thus increasing your portfolio's risk profile above where you intended it to be. As markets drop, the opposite can happen and your allocation to equities falls below your target. This can reduce the portfolio's long-term growth potential.

An in-built benefit of rebalancing is that you end up selling high and buying low, as investments that have done well will now make up a larger percentage of your portfolio than initially, and poorer performing investments will make up a lower proportion. If mean reversion occurs, you set up your portfolio to participate and benefit.

While it may seem like rebalancing is placing a contrarian slant on your portfolio management, it nonetheless removes emotive decision-making and provides a rule-based framework, which can be particularly useful during periods of volatility. If you forego rebalancing, you are essentially allowing the market to dictate your risk profile.

In practical terms, there are a few ways in which rebalancing can be executed. You could set a regular review period (e.g. quarterly, semi-annually, or annually) or rebalance when an asset class deviates from target by a certain percentage or more. You might also want to build in a mechanism for considering costs, such as transaction costs, or tax due, for example, on capital gains if positions are held outside tax wrappers. You can also use new portfolio contributions to effectively rebalance your portfolio by diverting them into the underweighted asset types of your portfolio, rather than outright selling down overweight positions.

INVESTMENT KNOWLEDGE

The greater your understanding of markets, how diversification works, and the drivers of long-term returns, the more confident an investor you become. That confidence can pay dividends during times of market stress when less confident investors can make costly emotional decisions. Understanding risk and return is key – in particular, that higher returns come with higher volatility. When building this knowledge, it can pay to focus on educational aspects of investing (such as quality books) as opposed to daily coverage in the financial media. Understand how different assets move in relation to each other (i.e. asset class correlation) and how they behave in various economic environments that you are likely to encounter during your investment career.

Understanding compounding, and that the true benefits take a long time to really show themselves, is crucial here. Many investors grow impatient and interrupt the process, effectively hitting a hard reset on their long-term financial planning as a result.

CONTROLLING YOUR FINANCIAL DESTINY

There are many variables on your financial independence journey, and it's important to distinguish between factors you can control, or influence, and those that are beyond your control. Market cycles, investment returns, the state of the economy, and even how long you need your portfolio to endure are factors over which we have little control – we can only make educated guesses, based on historical averages, or reasonable assumptions.

That said, we can set ourselves up for success by focusing energy, and attention, on the many areas that are directly within your control: utilising your tax wrappers, managing costs, investing in your health, and avoiding lifestyle inflation.

Controlling what you can helps create a robust foundation to prepare for whatever the future brings. In this case, don't let trying to be perfect get in the way of taking good action on your future security.

NOTES

1 Stone, Robert *Personal Investments* (Straight Forward Publishing, 2015), page 120.
2 ING Think. "What Is the Diderot Effect?" (10 June 2020) (accessed 10 March 2026). https://think.ing.com/downloads/pdf/article/what-is-the-diderot-effect.
3 ISAs can be accessed earlier. As for tax considerations, when multiplying a series of numbers (representing contributions, investment returns, and identical effective tax rates) together, the exact ordering makes no difference mathematically by itself. The question centres more on the wider considerations surrounding the best tax year to move the tax point to. However, whether ISAs or pensions are right for your specific circumstances can be a more complex question than a quick rule of thumb can address.

REFERENCES

ING Think. "What Is the Diderot Effect?" (10 June 2020) (accessed 10 March 2026). https://think.ing.com/downloads/pdf/article/what-is-the-diderot-effect.

Stone, Robert *Personal Investments* (Straight Forward Publishing, 2015).

18

THE SECRET INGREDIENT TO FINANCIAL INDEPENDENCE

Saving for financial independence will never cost as little as it does if you start today. There is no financial benefit to delaying, and the amount it will require in total contributions is only going to go up.

Time may be the most potent variable in wealth accumulation – and perhaps the least appreciated. The FIRE (Financial Independence, Retire Early) movement places a heavy emphasis on elevated savings rates, justifiably so if timeline compression is your goal. The question individuals need to determine for themselves is the trade-off between lifestyle and timeline compression that they are most comfortable with. The more the timeline is compressed, the greater the lifestyle sacrifice needs to be.

Allowing time to work its magic can deliver equivalent – or even superior – results without lifestyle compression. Simply put, time itself provides mathematical leverage that other variables cannot replicate.

THE POWER OF STARTING EARLY

The good news is that if you're still young and want to retire at a normal retirement age, building sufficient wealth is not that big an ask. With a few reasonable assumptions and a relatively simple investing strategy, you can allow time to do most of the work for you. The mathematics is compelling: money invested in your 20s has four decades to compound, which is double the time that money invested in your 40s has to grow.

DOI: 10.4324/9781003792444-18

EXAMPLE

Rose is seeking to retire at the normal retirement age. She has determined that in addition to the full state pension, she requires £20,000 per year, gross, from her portfolio from that age.

Using the 4% rule she has calculated her financial independence number as being £500,000.

We can calculate the annual contribution amount required to reach the £500,000 target amount if we know the number of years that the portfolio will have to compound and make some assumptions regarding investment returns.

If we assume that returns are 5% per annum, we can multiply the annual contribution amount by the number of years to retirement for Rose, and then calculate the total contributions that she will have made over her entire working career (for illustrative purposes assuming a constant salary).

If Rose starts contributing at age 21, her portfolio will have 46 years' worth of compounding working for her until she reaches state retirement age. Taking account of compound portfolio growth, her annual net contributions needed to meet her £500,000 are only £2,964.10 (or £247.01 per month).

Using 2025/2026 UK income tax rates, her net monthly pay, assuming a £33,000 gross annual salary, changes from £2,212 per month to £2,014, assuming she is contributing these savings into a private pension. So, the actual monthly cost to her is £198 per month. This equates to a savings rate of almost 9%.

We can calculate how these numbers change depending on when her starting point is, and the number of years that she will have to compound her portfolio, until she reaches 67.

As we can see, starting early means Rose needs to save smaller amounts consistently over time.

Starting at age 21, she needs to make total contributions over her career that equate to less than a quarter of her target portfolio amount, and her savings rate can afford to be more modest. Given the long timescale available, her portfolio can rely heavily on compounding to achieve the rest.

Starting at age 51 removes this option, as there is far less time for compound growth to occur, and so she will have to contribute more

Table 18.1 Total contribution sizes by starting age

Starting Age	*Annual Contribution*	*SIPP Monthly Net Cost After Tax*	*Savings Rate*	*Years to Compound*	*Total Contributions*	*Contributions as % of Target Sum*
21	£2,964	£198	9%	46	£109,075	22%
31	£5,217	£348	16%	36	£150,250	30%
41	£9,782	£652	29%	26	£203,465	41%
51	£21,135	£1,438	65%	16	£276,100	55%

than half of the target portfolio size through saving. The overall impact on her savings rate is dramatic. Rose needs to run a savings rate seven times higher throughout her 50s and 60s up to retirement to reach her target.

THE TIME VS LIFESTYLE TRADE-OFF

Compounding let loose over an extended period can produce results that even aggressive savers with compressed timelines simply cannot match.

You can't just double the amount you are saving each month to get to your financial independence number twice as quickly. Compounding is exponential rather than linear; its full effect accelerates over time. Consider this example: assuming 7% investment rates, doubling your savings rates from 10% to 20% reduces your timeline to financial independence only from 42 to 31 years. Starting 11 years earlier could (on average) achieve the same result without any lifestyle compression needed at all. Importantly, due to how investment returns compound, the final decade of your investment journey can accumulate more absolute wealth than all previous decades combined.

If you have time on your side, the real magic of compound growth can be fully unleashed on your portfolio. This can act as a much more powerful force than the contribution size.

EXAMPLE: A TALE OF TWO INVESTORS

- Early Esther: starts investing £1,200 annually (£100 per month) at age 25 but stops at 35 having made £12,000 total contributions over 10 years.
- Late Larry: Starts investing £1,200 annually at age 35, continuing until 65. Over 30 years his total contributions are £36,000.

Assuming 7% annual returns:

Esther's portfolio at 65 = £126,209.19
Larry's portfolio at 65 = £113,352.94

Larry's portfolio hasn't quite caught up with Esther's, despite Larry having made three times the contributions as Esther over a much more protracted period. The early start and extra 10 years of compound growth have given her portfolio an unassailable advantage.

Key lessons:

- Starting early is your greatest asset when building wealth.
- Compound growth starts slowly but can accelerate dramatically

EXAMPLE: MICKEY'S STORY – THE POWER OF PATIENCE

Mickey is aiming to build a £1,000,000 fund to FIRE in about 15 years. He is expecting investment real returns to be around 5%. He calculates needing to save 50% of his net pay.

If investment returns turned out to be 7%, Mickey could actually retire in about 13.5 years with his 50% savings rate.

If Mickey dropped his savings rate to just 20% but focused on leaving a legacy rather than early retirement, his investment pot could be more than double his FIRE target number, in real terms, within 38 years, despite his far more modest 20% savings rate.

If time is the secret ingredient, then patience and discipline are what you need to utilise it. Patient investors, even with more moderate but consistent savings rates, can achieve superior long-term outcomes over extended timeframes compared to the intense compression techniques many FIRE strategies employ.

BEYOND THE NUMBERS: ADDITIONAL ADVANTAGES

There are many other advantages to letting time do the work, not least that it can be psychologically easier to maintain a moderate savings rate for longer than a more aggressive savings rate for a compressed timeline.

Career-wise, many FIRE adherents retire before reaching peak earning capacity. As individuals climb career ladders, they often find themselves in higher-paying, progressively more satisfying roles.

Career capital can compound much like financial capital, with early sacrifices translating into promotion opportunities. The financial impact can be dramatic, resulting in late-career income bursts that accelerate wealth beyond what high savings rates, and early career sacrifices, could ever achieve. Career advancement can also form a natural hedge against inflation, creating superior real returns. Extended careers increase exposure to financial windfalls through advancement opportunities, business ventures, and investment insights. Thus, the longer your financial journey, the more you're exposed to positive surprises.

Extended time horizons come with the added benefit that they can reduce the risks of a financial independence strategy failing. One reason for this is that the period a portfolio needs to cover is reduced in duration, but another is that by exposing capital to financial markets for a longer duration, average returns are more likely to look like their long-term trend. The shorter the timeframe, the greater the risk of outlying movements distorting the whole, particularly during periods of market distress, or an extended period of a poor sequence of returns.

In fact, an extended investment horizon can bring with it greater exposures to what futurists call "the technological tailwind effect" – the possibility of innovation, such as AI, creating productivity improvements and presenting investment opportunities that compound over time. The longer an investment time horizon, the more likely it is to ride these waves, in some cases multiple waves.

Investment knowledge also compounds. Experience creates progressively better decision-making, generating compound effects that compressed FIRE timelines may often go without.

By accepting longer time horizons, patient investors can expand lifestyle options that aggressive FIRE savers must forgo. This might involve upgrading lifestyle through increased spending while maintaining similar financial trajectories.

Perhaps one of the greatest benefits of extended financial independence timelines is a financial resilience dividend, in the form of the ability to adapt to changing circumstances. This includes wholesale lifestyle changes, due to new personal priorities, or simply due to market conditions. FIRE strategies may require rigid savings requirements due to the compressed timeline, and so can lack this level of adaptability.

The most important thing to keep sight of is that the plan is akin to a marathon and not a sprint. Small and consistent efforts can, and will, compound over time. The longer your horizon, the smaller the adjustments needed to get back on track or tweak your plan.

THE CASE FOR FRONT-LOADING SAVINGS

Many individuals start with modest retirement savings, only seriously looking at retirement planning later. Patrick Grant emphasises a sobering reality: "[A]ll too often, people wake up to the need to build a pension fund when it is too late. When a person is young, the last thing they want to be thinking about is saving for their old age."[1]

This makes sense from the point of view of early-career financial demands: repayment of student loans, property deposits, weddings, raising children – these can all take priority over what can seem like a distant goal. When these financial demands recede, individuals may be mid-career and possibly at their earning peak. This means that they can afford to run a much higher savings rate and "catch-up" (unless they have really left it very late). At this point, though, they may have no choice but to rely on their savings rate to achieve financial independence by retirement age. As Grant warns: "one thing is for certain and that is if you leave it too late then you will have to put away a large slice of your income to produce a decent pension."[2]

An alternative view argues for restructuring traditional career-stage advice by front-loading savings during early career stages. To illustrate why this can be so powerful, consider the value of £1 invested at various ages by the standard retirement age, 67. At a 7% real annual return, a pound invested at age 21 will compound to an impressive £22.47 in today's money – and is about 15 times more than the power of a pound invested at age 61:

Real value of each £1 invested at various ages:[3]

At Age	*Value at Retirement*
21	£22.47
31	£11.42
41	£5.81
51	£2.95
61	£1.50

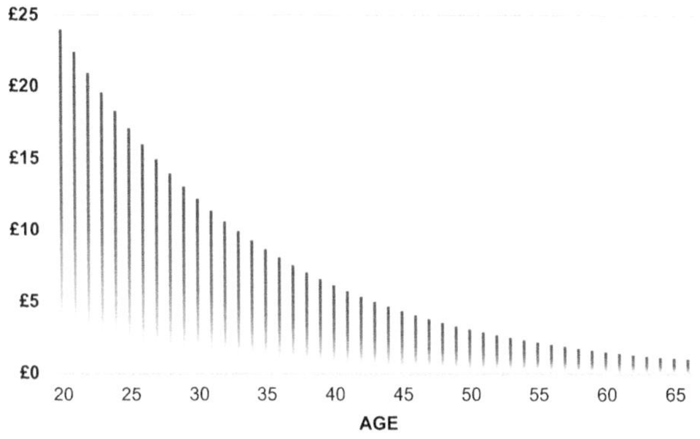

Figure 18.1 Graph showing value at retirement of each pound invested at various ages

As stated at the beginning of Chapter 4, the answer to the "how much" question for portfolio size "can throw up sums of money that can seem intimidating." However, how much we actually have to save towards our goal depends on how soon we can set aside each pound.

EXAMPLE

Someone targeting £1 million only needs to invest just under £44,500 if they achieve 7% real returns and can invest that amount at age 21 (and the £44,500 would reach the £1 million under its own power by standard retirement age).[4]

As we have examined, compound interest is exponential in nature. Early in the process, most gains come from making contributions rather than from interest growth. Investment returns appear modest and relatively linear in nature. However, given time, interest grows to the point that it exceeds capital contributions to the portfolio, and eventually the interest-on-interest component alone will also exceed the total contributions made. This is when the power of compounding becomes fully exposed.

Yoram Lustig provides crucial insight into how time works in your favour:

> [W]hen beginning saving for retirement, the amount you save is by far the most important aspect ... over the long term, however, investment returns have a big influence on the final outcome ...[5] in some years, returns are high ... in others they are low .... the larger the number of years, the higher the chances of hitting the average yearly return.[6]

Over the long term, the natural short-term volatility of the market will average out closer to historical norms.

EXAMPLE

Consider Dora, who starts investing £300 per month at age 25, versus Craig, who only starts investing the same amount at age 35. Assuming 7% annual returns, Dora ends up with £718,686 (from £144,000 in contributions made over 40 years) and Craig with £340,058 (from £108,000 in contributions made over 30 years). The extra 10 years of compounding more than doubled the size of Dora's portfolio versus Craig's.

CONCLUSION

It seems patience really is a virtue, and for those willing (and able) to employ it as a financial strategy, time itself can be unleashed as perhaps the most powerful ally on the road to financial freedom – one whose contribution to portfolio growth can grow exponentially over the years. If there is a secret ingredient to investing, it is time. The old adage about time in the market as opposed to trying to time the market really is true.

The FIRE movement has made invaluable contributions to the world of personal finance by highlighting the power of savings rates, particularly in compressing traditional retirement timelines. However, for investors focused on financial independence rather than the earliest possible retirement, time remains the silent partner that ultimately delivers the wealth-generating miracle of compound growth.

NOTES

1 Grant, Patrick *Personal Pensions & The Pensions Industry* (Straight Forward Publishing, 2022), page 13.
2 Grant, Patrick *Personal Pensions & The Pensions Industry* (Straight Forward Publishing, 2022), page 23.
3 FV = P(1 + r)^t (see Chapter 6).
4 1,000,000 / 22.47 = 44,499.
5 Lustig, Yoram *Saving and Investing for Retirement. The Definitive Handbook to Securing Your Financial Future* (Financial Times Guides, Pearson, 2016), page 32.
6 Lustig, Yoram *Saving and Investing for Retirement. The Definitive Handbook to Securing Your Financial Future* (Financial Times Guides, Pearson, 2016), page 34.

REFERENCES

Grant, Patrick *Personal Pensions & The Pensions Industry* (Straight Forward Publishing, 2022).

Lustig, Yoram *Saving and Investing for Retirement. The Definitive Handbook to Securing Your Financial Future* (Financial Times Guides, Pearson, 2016).

19

FROM THEORY TO PRACTICE

The tools and rules of thumb we have explored thus far allow you to customise your own strategy, considering your individual circumstances, and give you a general target to aim for. What that can look like in practice is the subject of the next section. This can be refined later and stress-tested with a fully fledged financial plan and modelling, and necessary adjustments made.

THE "PORTFOLIO ONLY" APPROACH

Before we get started, it is important to remind ourselves that the 4% rule is designed to show the initial safe withdrawal rate from a portfolio, which can then be adjusted for inflation in each subsequent year. Traditionally, when applied by FIRE practitioners, this often does not explicitly include pension income. There are some sound reasons for this, beyond simplicity. One is it better reflects the true financial burden of retiring early. Some FIRE adherents aim to retire in their 40s (or even before), and this can be decades before they can get access to pensions. If the point is to be 100% self-reliant, and fully financially independent, ignoring pensions can make some sense, as well as providing a potential financial safety net later in life.

Eligibility for the state pension might be subject to policy changes anyway, and saving into a private pension alongside FIRE-ing at the earliest opportunity might not be practical.

While, the state pension itself is unlikely to disappear, qualification criteria might substantially change (such as needing 35 years of contributions), the retirement age might be lifted, or it could become means-tested.

DOI: 10.4324/9781003792444-19

Many retirees in the UK are already not qualifying for the full state pension.[1] If someone is taking extreme early retirement, apart from the risk of the rules changing, whether they will make enough voluntary contributions to ensure they fully qualify is also something worth considering. If it is possible to live entirely by your own means for decades, some might even ask whether a pension might not just be a "bonus" or an additional "safety net" as opposed to representing a primary source of funding.

Certain other individuals may live in a jurisdiction where they might not be eligible for a state pension at all.

In these cases, and any others where a portfolio is solely responsible for funding life after work (i.e. there are no other income sources considered), you can directly focus on the interplay between your savings rate (and by extension your spending rate), expected average investment returns, and the portfolio withdrawal rate.

It becomes possible to analyse these variables purely in terms of the percentages involved and the mathematical relationships between them, regardless of the absolute figures for income, savings, and expenditure levels. Given some of the variables involved, some individuals may simply prefer to rely on this method when setting a landing area for their portfolios at retirement.

This is the approach[2] taken in the first part of this chapter's analysis. Individual profiles have been created based on varying percentage splits between current spending and saving, assuming these spending levels are maintained into retirement. The object is to show, through these examples, what the implications might be for someone solely reliant on their portfolio to support their retirement, following a similar strategy. We'll then use the profiles to show how some tweaks to them could affect the outcomes.

THE PASSIVE INCOME INTEGRATION CHALLENGE

For those qualifying for a full state pension, the financial independence question can eventually look very different from those who are entirely reliant on their portfolio.

In the UK, the full state pension is a flat amount. In the 2025/2026 tax year, the new full UK State Pension was £11,973 per year.[3] This creates different strategic considerations for lower-income earners (where the state pension eventually may cover 40–60% of retirement expenses – dramatically reducing the required portfolio size) than for higher-income earners (where the state pension may cover only 15–25% of retirement expenses, meaning the portfolio still bears most of the responsibility).

In both cases, including the state pension allows you to significantly downsize the required portfolio size because you need only 25 times the amount not covered by the state pension. (This can save an impressive £299,325 from the portfolio size when applying the 4% rule – 25 × £11,973.) For almost everyone (who works for a living), this will have a material impact. Qualification for the state pension can mean that leaving the state pension as a mere "safety net" for very early retirees means that withdrawals based on the 4% rule might end up far "safer" than would be otherwise necessary. Yet suggestions such as a pensionable age of 74, which an Institute for Fiscal Studies (IFS) study floated "would be needed if the state pension Triple Lock continued indefinitely," serve to underline why a degree of caution can be warranted on how the state pension features in plans.[4]

In any case, the state pension and other passive income streams introduce complexity versus the percentage-based calculations, which need to be addressed somehow in our assumptions.

One quick workaround is to apply the withdrawal amount to fund "excess expenditure" only, i.e. the proportion of spending that is not covered by other passive income sources.[5]

This approach is generally more suitable for scenarios where an individual is looking at retirement at the statutory retirement age – as the portfolio doesn't cover the portion of expenditure to be funded by the state pension at all in the interim.

The state pension won't be available at the point of an early retirement, and so in such cases a gap period is created that needs to be bridged. There are a few ways of doing this (if necessary):

1 Some individuals may prefer simply to modify the savings-to-expense ratios by the level of individual pension coverage, then continue using the percentage-based formulas as is to determine the general landing area for their portfolio.
2 Alternatively, while not ideal, assuming that an individual will continue to earn part-time income (equivalent to the state pension) until the state pension kicks in is also a practical compromise for now, if partial retirement is an option.

3 Another option is to perform a separate calculation for how much additional portfolio funds are needed to cover the bridging period, with the intention that a separate portfolio bucket is created to augment the main portfolio. This would provide funding (at a higher drawdown rate, as it is for the interim period only) effectively replacing the state pension for the bridging period until the state pension itself becomes accessible. Using a withdrawal rate of 8–9% for 15 years, without adjusting for inflation, for example, over the most recent 50 years, would, according to the Trinity Study, give close to a 100% success rate for stock-dominated portfolios – or 6–7% over the last 70 years.[6]

This noted, the analysis in the second part of this chapter shows different concrete income levels, using 2025/2026 tax rates and the UK State Pension levels, as examples (in addition to the portfolio-only approach), illustrating an "excess expenditure" approach. This takes account of the full UK State Pension but not how the bridging period is financed, so it is best used when considering retirement at the statutory retirement age.

PART I: PROFILE-BASED (PERCENTAGE) ANALYSIS

Perhaps the best starting point, though, is underlining (again) a simple fact: the mathematical reality of compound growth means that investing at the commencement of someone's career versus mid-career (or later) doesn't just change the timeline; it changes the entire strategic approach required.

The age at which we begin serious financial independence planning fundamentally alters the required savings rate, investment strategy, and realistic timeline expectations. To delve deeper into what this can mean in practice, let's consider concrete examples. In doing so, we consider five distinct saver profiles, which provide actionable insights and specific recommendations tailored to each profile.

Each of the five "profiles" set out below is an amalgam, resulting from an informal survey of 50 people from my network. Many are Treasury or other professionals, but some are simply old friends with an interest in finance who brought a slightly different perspective.

These profiles are not (designed to be) exhaustive by any means. The object is to illustrate how you might go about customising the techniques we have explored to your personal circumstances, rather than attempting to set up concrete profiles for you to follow instead of doing this.

A) THE "BALANCED OPTIMISER" PROFILE

KEY CHARACTERISTICS

- Began meaningful retirement saving around age 30
- Maintains a savings rate between 15–19% of income
- Generally, keeps a budget and is aware of their savings rate
- Has some form of financial plan in place
- Is actively saving for retirement

Balanced Optimisers (representing one-sixth of the survey cohort) occupy a pragmatic middle-path: neither starting serious long-term financial planning very early, nor delaying it until mid-career. They balance present enjoyment with future security, while neither saving minimally nor pursuing extreme frugality. It is likely such individuals may have spent their 20s establishing themselves in a career, which by 30 has led to a stabilised income that has increased to the level at which they can begin long-term saving and investing without needing to make extreme lifestyle sacrifices.

SCENARIO ANALYSIS

- With a savings rate of 15%, years to financial independence range from 35 to 43 depending on whether investment returns are 5–7%. Assuming they are entirely reliant on their portfolio for retirement, Balanced Optimisers could expect to achieve financial freedom (assuming consistent averages throughout their careers) at 65–73 years of age.
- At the upper end of the savings rate (19%) range, the years to financial independence drop to 32–38 years (or retirement aged 62–68).

IMPLICATIONS AND STRATEGIC CONSIDERATIONS

- Starting long-term planning at 30 (even at the professionally recommended rate of 15%) may not enable early retirement, unless the savings rate is increased further or investment returns are exceptionally high.
- Each 2% increase in the savings rate has the power to reduce time to financial independence by 2 to 3 years. With a 7% average return, this could mean an additional 3 years of retirement at the statistically still healthy age range of 62 to 65.
- Asset allocation and investment strategy is a key consideration for this group: the difference in investment returns from 5% to 7% has a substantial impact. At a 15% savings rate it translates to 7.5 years of additional working at the lower rate of investment return.
- Higher returns will come with increased volatility and risk, so the Balanced Optimiser will need to carefully consider their risk appetite. They should also pay careful consideration to managing fees and expenses, and taxes (by holding investments in tax-efficient accounts).
- Balanced Optimisers could consider allocating a larger proportion of any future pay rises to increased savings rather than inflating lifestyle. Any windfalls, inheritances, tax refunds, or bonuses could be used to bolster their investment pot.
- They could also consider strategic career moves, such as through education, to increase earnings potential, or develop additional income streams.

ADVANTAGES OF BEING A BALANCED OPTIMIZER

- Reduced lifestyle sacrifice while building wealth, minimising the risk of savings "fatigue"
- Maintaining flexibility to accommodate major life changes without derailing their financial independence plan
- Allowing for a longer runway to shape financial habits rather than needing to make dramatic changes overnight

B) THE "AUTO-ENROLLED (EARLY) STARTER" PROFILE

KEY CHARACTERISTICS

- Began retirement saving early in their careers (typically between ages 22 and 27)
- Maintains a savings rate between 1–8% of income (probably at the statutory minimum 8% pension auto-enrolment rate)
- Generally keeps a budget and is aware of their savings rate
- Has some form of financial plan in place
- Is actively saving for retirement, albeit at the statutory minimum rate

For Auto-Enrolled Starters (representing approximately one-quarter of the survey cohort), retirement saving begins with their entry into the workforce – primarily through the UK's auto-enrolment system. This cohort typically sticks with the statutory minimum: 8% in total, i.e. 5% from the employee and 3% from the employer. While the saving ratio might be considered modest, time is a key ally. This cohort is largely composed of recent graduates and young professionals. Although many in this category maintain budgets and demonstrate some financial awareness, their current priorities are lifestyle-focused, relying on the power of time and compounding to lay the foundation for their future security.

SCENARIO ANALYSIS

- Assuming they are entirely reliant on their portfolio for retirement, an 8% savings rate will mean financial independence in 45 years with a 7% investment return (and 56 years with a 5% return), translating to a retirement age of 67 (or 78) if saving is begun at age 22 (or 5 years later if starting at age 27).

IMPLICATIONS AND STRATEGIC CONSIDERATIONS

- Auto-enrolment early is a useful foundation to have, but by itself is unlikely to be adequate to fund an early retirement or perhaps even a comfortable one.

- Starting early may lead to a "set and forget" attitude or an assumption that the auto-enrolment amount must be adequate. Instead, this should be viewed merely as a starting point.
- An incremental improvement in the savings rate can have a large impact given the extended timelines at play. Increasing the savings rate from 8% to 10%, could reduce time to financial independence by 5 years at a 5% return, or 3 years at 7% (due to the already shorter timeframe with a 7% return at the original savings rate of 8%; there are fewer years compounding to make a difference).
- Auto-Enrolled Starters could consider gradual contribution increases and implement a savings escalator after pay rises. They could establish automatic contribution increases tied to pay rises.
- Other possibilities include investigating whether employers offer matching pension contributions above the statutory minimum (many do). Not only might this help to increase the savings rate, but the additional employer contributions can be viewed as essentially "free money."
- Auto-Enrolled Starters should also review investment allocations. Due to the long time scale involved, they are more likely to be able to afford to pursue more aggressive growth strategies, with time to ride out market volatility, particularly in the early years of their investment journey.
- Auto-Enrolled Starters should also focus on developing financial literacy alongside career development.

ADVANTAGES OF BEING AN AUTO-ENROLLED STARTER

- Auto-Enrolled Starters can harness the long-term power of compound growth throughout their careers. Even with a modest starting contribution, the longer timeline can mean that their portfolio can grow a lot over the coming decades, potentially even outperforming those making larger contributions but starting much later.
- The extended timeline can lower the pressure to save more aggressively, allowing for greater lifestyle flexibility – particularly in the face of life events. This can provide psychological support as well as establish positive financial habits early.
- The auto-enrolment system provides an effortless entry to the world of pension saving.

C) THE "LATE AWAKENER" PROFILE

KEY CHARACTERISTICS

- Began retirement saving later in their careers (typically late 30s or early 40s)
- Maintains a savings rate between 1–14% of income (still below the 15% recommended by Independent Financial Advisor – IFAs)
- May have some budget awareness but often underestimates the required savings rate
- May or may not have some form of financial plan
- Has become more actively engaged with retirement planning, albeit later than optimal

Late Awakeners (representing approximately one-quarter of the survey cohort) recognised the importance of serious retirement planning only later in their careers, perhaps as the result of a financial wake-up call, or the reaching of a life milestone. Many are now seeking to make up for lost time but face a challenging mathematical reality, seeking to balance the constraints of an established lifestyle and other financial commitments with reaching an appropriate savings rate. The combination of late start and suboptimal savings rate represents a twin challenge to even achieving traditional financial independence timelines at normal retirement age.

SCENARIO ANALYSIS

- For someone solely reliant on their portfolio, even with a 14% savings rate, years to financial independence range from 36 to 44 depending on whether investment returns are 5% or 7%.
- For a Late Awakener starting retirement saving at age 40, the chances of a portfolio needing to last 30 years in retirement becomes more unlikely, as freedom itself may come later. This being the case, perhaps their portfolio withdrawal rate could be safely increased, meaning that a smaller overall portfolio size is needed to finance an unchanged withdrawal amount. With a 5% withdrawal rate, years to financial independence fall to 33–40 (or 31–37 at 6%).

- At an 8% savings rate, 39–48 working years would still be needed even with a 6% withdrawal rate, demonstrating the mathematical reality facing Late Awakeners.

IMPLICATIONS AND STRATEGIC CONSIDERATIONS

- Among immediate priorities, for Late Awakeners, is aggressively increasing their savings rate, even at the cost of significant lifestyle adjustments, to the extent that this is possible. To reach financial independence at age 67, for someone now 40, they would need a 25% savings rate (with a 4% withdrawal rate) even with a 7% average investment return.
- To help achieve this, Late Awakeners could look at maximising pension tax advantages, utilising tax breaks from paying into private pensions – to bump their savings rate, prioritise eliminating any high-interest debt, and even consider downsizing or relocating to reduce housing costs.
- Tax advantages in the UK tax system can provide returns that no stock market can match. Late Awakeners may need to save more but the tax breaks on pension contributions (and even the ability to carry some of these forward between tax years) mean that the taxman to some extent bears the burden of lost compound growth.
- For someone solely reliant on their portfolio (and unable to take advantage of these tax levers) with a projected financial independence age that exceeds normal life expectancy, Late Awakeners will likely need to pull multiple financial levers: increasing their savings rate, optimising investment returns, extending working years, and even then reconsidering what financial independence for them looks like – possibly factoring in only a partial retirement strategy with some part-time work continuing until later.
- Late Awakeners should probably also look at income-maximising strategies such as career advancement and side businesses.
- Among immediate priorities is aggressively increasing their savings rate, even at the cost of significant lifestyle adjustments, to the extent that this is possible. To reach financial independence at age 67, for someone now 40, they would need a 25%

savings rate (with a 4% withdrawal rate) even with a 7% average investment return.

- To help achieve this, Late Awakeners could look at maximising pension tax advantages, utilising tax breaks from paying into private pensions – to bump their savings rate, prioritise eliminating any high-interest debt, and even consider downsizing or relocating to reduce housing costs.

ADVANTAGES OF BEING A LATE AWAKENER

- As Late Awakeners are mid-career individuals, many may have reached higher earning potential with a clear understanding of career potential and may have made significant progress on major family formation expenses – such as home purchases and child-rearing – which could free up funds going forward for retirement saving.
- Despite not having focused on retirement savings specifically, many Late Awakeners may nonetheless have accumulated assets such as equity in their home, which they can also potentially utilise for retirement planning purposes.
- While the mathematical reality can't be denied, Late Awakeners may also have heightened motivation, despite the later start, and can use this to significantly improve their retirement prospects with prompt decisive action.

D) THE "DEDICATED ACCUMULATOR" PROFILE

KEY CHARACTERISTICS

- Began meaningful retirement saving between age 30 and 40
- Maintains a high savings rate between 20 and 30% of income
- Has a financial plan in place and demonstrates financial literacy and engagement

Although Dedicated Accumulators (representing approximately one-sixth of the survey cohort) didn't start saving at the start of their careers, working with a high savings rate means that they are able to make up some lost ground (particularly those starting at the lower end of the age range). The high savings ratio and time available act as a powerful wealth-building engine and mean these individuals can still achieve financial independence by their late 50s to mid-60s, meaning significant lifestyle flexibility remains possible in their 50s and beyond.

Dedicated Accumulators allocate a substantial proportion of their net income to long-term wealth building but still manage to maintain a balanced approach to present-day enjoyment.

SCENARIO ANALYSIS

- With a savings rate of 20%, the years to financial independence range from 31 to 37 depending on whether investment returns are 5–7%; or 25–29 years at a 29% savings rate.
- At the upper end of the savings rate range (i.e. at 29%), assuming they are entirely reliant on their portfolio for retirement, Dedicated Accumulators could expect to achieve financial freedom at 55–64 or 64–68 years old.

IMPLICATIONS AND STRATEGIC CONSIDERATIONS

- Dedicated Accumulators can still achieve portfolio growth that meaningfully contributes to compounding. They should remain cognisant of the milestones towards financial independence, such as when compounding makes a more meaningful contribution to their portfolio growth.
- Their savings rate is still low enough that across-the-board frugality is not a necessity, and so Dedicated Accumulators can focus on optimising spending to maximise life satisfaction.
- Financial independence before traditional retirement age is possible and can reward Dedicated Accumulators with significant lifestyle flexibility in their 50s and early 60s. However, at such ages, there is a gap between financial independence being achieved and state pension eligibility, meaning any portfolio drawdown plan must take account of this.
- Individuals could consider their purpose beyond financial independence, strategically investing in skills, credentials and experiences that not only enhance their career but that could be useful post-independence, potentially for second careers, or creative pursuits.

- Dedicated accumulators should also consider enhancing risk management strategies, including appropriate insurance coverage, emergency reserves, and portfolio stress-testing.

ADVANTAGES OF BEING A DEDICATED ACCUMULATOR

- Dedicated Accumulators' substantial savings rates create the possibility for tax optimisation (such as making greater utilisation of pension contributions) and tapping stocks and shares ISA allowances, much more than those with a lower savings rate.
- Starting at age 30 (although missing out on the earliest years of compounding) creates a decent investment base due to the high savings rate and tax breaks. This can generate significant compounding returns, and this can reduce financial stress to a great degree.
- As portfolios grow, Dedicated Accumulators' flexibility increases either for early retirement or making career decisions based on factors outside of compensation alone.

E) THE "FREEDOM ACCELERATOR" PROFILE

KEY CHARACTERISTICS:

- Began meaningful retirement saving very early in their careers (in any case before age 29, but typically early/mid-20s)
- Maintains an exceptionally high savings rate of at least 30%, but frequently over 50%.
- Has a comprehensive, detailed financial plan in place; is actively and strategically
- pursuing early financial independence and demonstrates exceptional financial literacy and engagement

Freedom Accelerators (representing approximately one-sixth of the survey cohort) are the intentional architects of early freedom, deliberately designing and building a path to get them there. This cohort has two very powerful financial forces working for them: an exceptionally high savings rate and an early start – to create a path that can take them to financial freedom decades earlier than the traditional retirement age. Unlike peers who entered the workforce and immediately focused on lifestyle expansion, Freedom Accelerators began wealth building from the very beginnings of their careers.

SCENARIO ANALYSIS

- With a savings rate of 30%, years to financial independence range from 24 to 28 depending on whether investment returns are 5–7%. Assuming they are entirely reliant on their portfolio for retirement, they could expect to achieve financial freedom (assuming consistent averages throughout their careers) at 49–53 years of age – even if starting from 25.
- At a 50% savings rate, the timeline drops drastically to 15–17 years to financial independence, so a Freedom Accelerator could even reach that goal at age 40. However, even with no investment returns at all, the power of their savings rate alone means financial independence is achievable in 25 years (after 17 years with a 60% savings rate or even 11 years at 70%).

Factoring in a 7% return with the 70% savings rates could see Freedom Accelerator already financially independent after just 8 years of working.

IMPLICATIONS AND STRATEGIC CONSIDERATIONS

- Freedom Accelerators can realistically achieve financial independence 20 or 25 years before traditional retirement age, creating unprecedented life flexibility in their 40s and beyond.
- This can create a unique psychological challenge as Freedom Accelerators could be ready to transition to post-financial independence at a time when most of their peer group are deeply engaged in traditional career paths and at their earnings peak.
- With early retirement, longevity planning could be a concern, as Freedom Accelerators need to plan for their portfolio to last for far longer than traditional retirements – potentially over five decades. At the same time there is a long gap potentially to state pension entitlement (which in itself is not a given unless a Freedom Accelerator actively chooses to keep contributing towards it).

- The savings rate will likely be the dominant factor in determining the timeline to freedom, more so than income level or investment returns. However, due to longevity considerations, investment portfolios should be constructed accordingly, possibly using a bucket approach for different life phases such as for early retirement (another bucket for once SIPPS (Self-Invested Personal Pensions) can be accessed or the state pension kicks in) and for the ultra-long-term (later retirement, provision of potential care fees, or legacy planning).
- Higher equity allocations and other long-term growth assets should be considered for longer horizons, and traditional portfolio de-risking strategies (where the equity element is reduced prior to drawdown) could look very different with a higher equity portion sustained for longer. This is also likely to be a consideration where legacy planning is an intention, to maximize the long-term benefits of the power of compounding.
- Freedom Accelerators could consider income maximisation and periods of intense career focus in their 20s and 30s with the explicit goal to create options for significant deceleration by their early 40s. If such is a consideration, career selection can take on a strategic dimension where high income and reasonable lifestyle demands might take priority over more traditional considerations like interest or passion. This could incorporate geographic arbitrage such as relocating to high-income, low-tax jurisdictions during the accumulation phase, and/or to retirement in lower-cost areas.
- It is important to recognise that some individuals maintaining savings rates at this level may be doing so for purposes other than savings for financial independence, such as trying to get on the property ladder. To this end some may even be living at home to enable them to do so. Those doing so should remain cognisant of the dangers of lifestyle inflation subsequently.
- For those who have designed lifestyles around being able to maintain savings rates at such elevated levels, it is certainly worth considering the rationale behind this. To avoid too much deprivation, Freedom Accelerators could, instead, focus on designing a lifestyle that can be maintained both before and

after achieving financial independence, and considering clear purpose, structure, and meaning for post-financial independence life.
- Psychological challenges should also be heavily considered upfront: potentially focusing on developing skills, such as creative pursuits, during the accumulation phase.

ADVANTAGES OF BEING A FREEDOM ACCELERATOR

- Being a Freedom Accelerator provides extraordinary lifestyle flexibility. By potentially compressing whole careers into 15–20 years instead of 40–45 years, Freedom Accelerators can radically reduce their lifetime work requirement.
- This can open up decades of life for alternate pursuits, second careers, travel, family time, or other priorities. The combination of an early start and high savings rate creates a huge compounding engine and resilience to financial shocks that life can throw up.
- For those wishing to continue to work, the option of being able to suddenly stop or dramatically reduce working hours can create substantial psychological benefits as well as negotiating power.

If you find yourself strongly drawn to a certain profile, this might denote your starting point rather than having to be your destination, i.e. it is certainly possible to move between them. In fact, the most successful financial independence journeys might strategically combine elements from across the profiles:

- The Auto-Enrolled Starter's early start
- Freedom Accelerator's savings discipline
- Dedicated Accumulator's commitment
- Balanced Optimiser's pragmatism
- Late Awakener's determination

PART II: INCOME LEVEL ANALYSIS: HOW SALARY AFFECTS YOUR PATH TO FINANCIAL INDEPENDENCE

Fortunately, for those in most of the above profiles, in many cases we are not solely reliant just on our portfolios. State pensions can make a meaningful difference, not to mention the fact that any of the variables in this simple modelling can change over time (and probably will).

In the section below, let's add in some practical nuance by showing how different income levels affect financial independence timelines concretely. Given the role the state pension can have, percentage-based calculations may prove to be overly conservative here.

Let's start by looking at a specific step-by-step example (for simplicity assuming all savings come from post-tax income), and then employ the same methodology for the other scenarios shown in each of the tables throughout this section.

All calculations assume a 5% annual investment return.

In each case, the years to financial independence are rounded up.

EXAMPLE: STEP BY STEP

- £33,000 gross income (£26,548 after tax)

With a savings rate: 8%

- Annual savings = £26,548 × 0.08 = £2,123.84
- Annual expenses = £26,548 - £2,123.84 = £24,424.16
- Financial independence need (per annum) = £24,424.16

Portfolio only:

- 4% – Gross FI number = £24,424.16 × 25 = £610,604
- Years to financial independence (total) = 56

Excess Expenditure-Level Analysis

- Financial independence need (per annum) incl. state pension = £24,424.16 - £11,973 = £12,451.16
- 4% – Gross FI number incl. state pension = £12,451.16 × 25 = £311,279
- Years to financial independence (total) incl. state pension = 44

Someone qualifying for the full state pension and intending to retire at the statutory retirement age will need to start saving 8% of net income 44 years before – assuming all parameters remain constant. Alternatively, they could shift to part-time work after 44 years of working and continue this until they qualify for the State Pension.

Key insights: For income earners in this band, the state pension provides significant relief – covering 49% of expenses at the 8% savings rate and an impressive 90% at the 50% savings rate. However, even when expenses are minimised, there remains a basic cost of living level below which it is not possible to push expenses (we need to eat and have somewhere to sleep, for example). These costs disproportionately impact individuals the lower their income is. In practice, maintaining a high savings rate may not be feasible for many due to these unavoidable expenses.

Key insight: For income earners in this bracket, the state pension covers 34% of expenses at the 8% savings rate and 63% at the 50% savings rate. While this remains significant, it is less dramatic compared to the lower-income earners in the first table. The basic cost of living also represents a smaller proportion of net income, making

Table 19.1 At £33,000 gross income (£26,548 after tax)

Savings Rate	*Annual Savings*	*Annual Expenses*	*FI Number (Total)*	*FI Number (After State Pension)*	*Years to FI (Total)*	*Years to FI (With State Pension)*
8%	£2,124	£24,424	£610,600	£311,279	56 years	44 years
15%	£3,982	£22,566	£564,145	£264,820	43 years	31 years
20%	£5,310	£21,238	£530,960	£231,635	37 years	24 years
30%	£7,964	£18,584	£464,590	£165,265	28 years	15 years
50%	£13,274	£13,274	£331,850	£32,525	17 years	3 years

Table 19.2 At £50,000 gross income (£38,076 after tax)

Savings Rate	*Annual Savings*	*Annual Expenses*	*FI Number (Total)*	*FI Number (After State Pension)*	*Years to FI (Total)*	*Years to FI (With State Pension)*
8%	£3,046	£35,030	£875,748	£576,423	56 years	49 years
15%	£5,711	£32,365	£809,115	£509,790	43 years	35 years
20%	£7,615	£30,461	£761,520	£462,195	37 years	29 years
30%	£11,423	£26,653	£666,330	£367,005	28 years	20 years
50%	£19,038	£19,038	£475,950	£176,625	17 years	8 years

Table 19.3 At £100,000 gross income (£64,735 after tax)

Savings Rate	*Annual Savings*	*Annual Expenses*	*FI Number (Total)*	*FI Number (After State Pension)*	*Years to FI (Total)*	*Years to FI (With State Pension)*
8%	£5,179	£59,556	£1,488,905	£1,189,580	56 years	52 years
15%	£9,710	£55,025	£1,375,619	£1,076,294	43 years	39 years
20%	£12,947	£51,788	£1,294,700	£995,375	37 years	30 years
30%	£19,421	£45,315	£1,132,875	£833,538	28 years	24 years
50%	£32,368	£32,368	£809,188	£509,863	17 years	12 years

higher savings rates more achievable. However, for those considering early retirement, their portfolio will still likely need to cover the pension amount until they reach the statutory retirement age or work part-time in the interim.

Key insight: For higher-income earners, the state pension covers only 20% of expenses at the 8% savings rate and 37% at the 50% savings rate. While this coverage remains meaningful, it is clear that savings rates have a much greater impact on achieving financial independence.

High-income earners must primarily rely on their own investments to reach financial independence, regardless of whether the goal is early retirement, or retiring at the statutory age.

Factoring in the state pension results in only a slightly shorter timeline.

WORKING BACKWARDS

Individuals could use the above tables to look at retirement age and work backwards when considering setting their savings rate, if they have the option to do so. Someone on a higher income may have more flexibility in this regard.

EXAMPLE

Someone intending to save 15% will find that they needed to have begun saving towards retirement by age 28.

If an individual is already 37, they would need to save a slightly higher 20%, consistently, to catch up.

SOME CONCLUSIONS

Hopefully, this chapter has helped you consider some ways to apply the theory from the rest of this book. The overall message might be that financial independence success comes from optimising savings rate, expense management, investment returns, and timeline simultaneously in your own circumstances.

We can also reinforce some general key takeaways from this analysis:

- Savings rate dominance: In seeking to achieve financial independence quickly, savings rates matter more than income levels. With a high savings rate, even those on modest incomes can achieve financial independence in compressed times, although running a high savings rate on more modest income levels is likely more challenging.
- Age compensation: Starting late necessitates running a higher savings rate, but it is never too late to improve your situation. The tax breaks available provide a powerful tailwind to make up for the loss of part of the compounding runway.
- State pension income: Factoring in state pensions can significantly reduce the required overall portfolio size, but the impact is more marked the lower an individual's income is.
- Lifestyle inflation costs: In fact, higher earners with low savings rates may struggle the most with challenges related to lifestyle inflation in the long term, as the state pension will cover a lower portion of their expenditure – and they will still need to amass a significant portfolio to cover their pre-existing expenditure after retirement.

TIMING CONSIDERATIONS AND CASH FLOW PLANNING

Within the scenarios covered in this chapter, there is a baked-in assumption that the variables remain roughly stable. That can be sufficient for determining the general landing area for our portfolio, but it necessitates revisiting calculations as and when one of the variables changes. It is a good idea anyway to recalibrate periodically (e.g. annually). There is, after all, time to tweak our plan before we get to our destination.

It is important to recognise, though, that the ask on our portfolio, in practice, is unlikely to be totally constant over time. We have looked at some ways around this to keep our assumptions simple.

Simplicity can come up against the challenges posed by reality. Some early retirees may consider a higher initial withdrawal rate, for instance, during the first phase of their retirement, for the "bridge period," until the state pension begins, and then switch to a lower rate to compensate. The portfolio might need to assume 100% responsibility for all expenses until the state pension becomes available (and a lower proportion after). In the meantime, if we really want financial independence to mean financial independence, using different withdrawal strategies over time eventually makes a comprehensive cash flow plan essential. Ideally, this will come soon enough that there is valuable time available to adjust the plan.

NOTES

1 Rickard Straus, Rachel "Half of Britons Miss Out on the Full State Pension – But Here's the ONE Easy Thing to Boost Yours" (*This Is Money*, 2 February 2026) (accessed 17 February 2026). https://www.thisismoney.co.uk/money/pensions/article-15519377/Video-Half-Britons-miss-state-pension-heres-ONE-easy-thing-boost-RACHEL-RICKARD-STRAUS.html.

2 This represents the practical application of the formulas set out in Chapter 7 of this book: *The Mathematics of Financial Independence*.

3 The full new UK State Pension, for those reaching state pension age on or after 6 April 2016 (requiring 35 qualifying years). Cooley, Philip L., Hubbard, Carl M., and Walz, Daniel T. "Retirement Savings: Choosing a Withdrawal Rate That Is Sustainable" (*American Association of Individual Investors Journal*, February 1998). https://www.gov.uk/new-state-pension/what-youll-get; Rickard Straus, Rachel "Half of Britons Miss Out on the Full State Pension – But Here's the ONE Easy Thing to Boost Yours" (This Is Money, 2 February 2026) (accessed 17 February 2026). https://www.thisismoney.co.uk/money/pensions/article-15519377/Video-Half-Britons-miss-state-pension-heres-ONE-easy-thing-boost-RACHEL-RICKARD-STRAUS.html.

4 The Open University "Speculation of State-Pension Retirement at 74? OU Expert Gives Us the Truth" (no date) (accessed 3 February 2026). https://www.open.ac.uk/blogs/news/arts-social-sciences/speculation-of-state-pension-retirement-at-74-ou-expert-gives-us-the-truth/.

5 By subtracting the expected pension amount from total annual expenses (and then multiplying the remaining excess expenditure by 25). Many in the FIRE community account for pensions in this way.

6 Tables 1and 2 in Cooley, Philip L., Hubbard, Carl M., and Walz, Daniel T. "Retirement Savings: Choosing a Withdrawal Rate That Is Sustainable"

(*American Association of Individual Investors Journal*, February 1998). https://www.gov.uk/new-state-pension/what-youll-get https://www.thisismoney.co.uk/money/pensions/article-15519377/Video-Half-Britons-miss-state-pension-heres-ONE-easy-thing-boost-RACHEL-RICKARD-STRAUS.html.

REFERENCES

Cooley, Philip L., Hubbard, Carl M., and Walz, Daniel T. "Retirement Savings: Choosing a Withdrawal Rate That Is Sustainable" (*American Association of Individual Investors Journal*, February 1998). https://www.gov.uk/new-state-pension/what-youll-get https://www.thisismoney.co.uk/money/pensions/article-15519377/Video-Half-Britons-miss-state-pension-heres-ONE-easy-thing-boost-RACHEL-RICKARD-STRAUS.html.

The Open University "Speculation of State-Pension Retirement at 74? OU Expert Gives Us the Truth" (no date) (accessed 3 February 2026). https://www.open.ac.uk/blogs/news/arts-social-sciences/speculation-of-state-pension-retirement-at-74-ou-expert-gives-us-the-truth/.

Rickard Straus, Rachel "Half of Britons Miss Out on the Full State Pension – But Here's the ONE Easy Thing to Boost Yours" (*This Is Money*, 2 February 2026) (accessed 17 February 2026). https://www.thisismoney.co.uk/money/pensions/article-15519377/Video-Half-Britons-miss-state-pension-heres-ONE-easy-thing-boost-RACHEL-RICKARD-STRAUS.html.

20

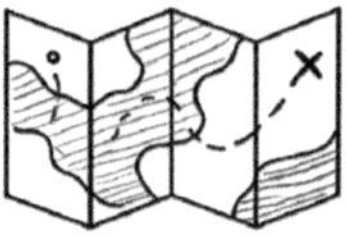

WEALTH ON AUTOPILOT

INVESTING MADE EASY

The Pareto Principle (also known as the 80/20 rule) has become a fundamental concept well beyond the world of economics. It is a powerful tool, as a guiding strategy for the distribution of resources, improving productivity, efficiency, and profitability. It works by highlighting the importance of focusing on the key factors to achieve the majority of results.

By identifying the 20% of tasks that contribute to 80% of the results, you can prioritise your efforts and focus on what really matters. A small portion of your investment activity will yield the most significant results in terms of your financial independence journey. In this chapter, let's recap the lessons of the previous chapters and then consider how these can be brought together into a simple, and Pareto-efficient, investing strategy.

PARETO EFFICIENCY IN INVESTMENT STRATEGY

The principle highlights the trade-off between the simplicity and cost-effectiveness of passive investing and the potential (but uncertain) higher returns of active management.

Purchasing a single global index fund is a great step in this direction, as it provides you with an instant diversified equity portfolio across a wide range of international markets. A global index fund is the ultimate "buy and forget" product. Combining investing in one with pound-cost averaging embodies Pareto efficiency perfectly: this single, simple strategy can deliver the majority of investment success with minimal effort, cost, and emotional stress.

DOI: 10.4324/9781003792444-20

A global index fund casts a wide net. Holding an index fund as a core element of your portfolio ensures you capture the winners; as you're backing the entire field, by definition, you participate in future gains without having to identify the individual stocks that they will come from. (Alternatively, you or the manager of any active funds you hold must find them.)

Market gains can be heavily concentrated, with overall performance driven by a small number of high-performing stocks. Recent themes include tech stocks (which have evolved from the so-called FAANGS[1] to the Magnificent Seven). The success of a large number of portfolios in recent years has been determined by whether they held these stocks in the right proportion – or not. Having an underweight exposure to this sector has meant in many, if not most, cases that portfolios have underperformed.

KEEPING IT SIMPLE

An investment plan can be straightforward and surprisingly simple. However, the temptation to tinker and do something more sophisticated can be equally hard to resist.

"Having a target asset allocation helps you to stay invested in order to take advantage of the mathematical power of compounding – which Albert Einstein described as the eighth wonder of the world."[2] Regular investing can benefit from cost savings, and these will compound over time.

Going on autopilot is one way of doing this. If you automate your investments through mechanisms like pound-cost averaging, that ensures you keep investing at the same pace no matter what's happening in the markets.

THE POWER OF SYSTEMATIC INVESTING

Pound-cost averaging can contribute significantly to the success of your investment story. Contributing regardless of whether the market is soaring or plunging can help harness higher highs, or get you into the market at the lows, likely at points when everything else is telling you to run. Sometimes pound-cost averaging may be the only tool that we have to do this.

John Kay argues in his book *The Long and the Short of It*:

> The effectiveness of pound cost averaging illustrates how low share prices are an opportunity rather than a problem for the intelligent investor. Conventional investors are usually excited when they hear that the market is going up, disappointed when they learn it has fallen. As Buffett has occasionally pointed out, this is odd.[3]

He goes further:

> [Pound-cost averaging] will, on average, outperform the market, and the more volatile the markets, the greater the gains ... it works through its built-in mechanism for buying more when prices are relatively low and less when prices are relatively high. No judgement is required by the investor that prices are relatively low or relatively high.[4]

The real power of a systematic approach is that it removes the emotional component from investment decisions. Committing to regular contributions to a diversified portfolio, regardless of market conditions, eliminates behavioural bias and the psychological traps that derail many investors.

THE COST OF INTERRUPTION

It's also important to remember that as the majority of compounded gains come in the latter stages of the investment journey, investors must stay patient and consistent. Any disruption to contributions being made, or investment strategy, can also compound. Automating the process of regular contributions has the benefit of removing the decision-making part of regular investing.

There are further steps we can take so as not to disrupt contributions, such as building a separate emergency fund (for example, the 3–6-month buffer) and taking out income protection insurance on top of this – or tapping the bond portion of portfolios before selling stocks.

We can keep in mind the lessons of market efficiency and trying to time the market and train ourselves to ignore market volatility, as short-term movements can translate to mere noise in the face of a decades-long plan. (Sometimes withdrawals may be necessary, but it's a good idea to consider these ahead of time and create clear decision rules to establish objective criteria for how to manage withdrawals if they are truly needed.)

Interrupting compounding carries mathematical penalties far exceeding the apparent cost. First, there's immediate loss of withdrawn amounts (or skipped contributions). Then there are future returns that would have been earned on them, plus future returns on those lost returns. This creates a compounding chain reaction, with each subsequent year compounding losses further.

Compounding can be interrupted in a number of ways:

- Direct portfolio withdrawals (before reaching portfolio goals) are one way. But there are several further errors to avoid.
- Exiting positions during market volatility or temporarily stopping regular investments is another.

However, there may be less appreciated interruptions:

- Excessive trading and rebalancing positions incur transaction costs (and potential tax consequences), which can also compound out into the future.
- Moving from growth assets to a more wealth preservation, and conservative, strategy too early could also have a significant impact, as the majority of returns come in the later years of compounding.

Sticking with a plan to compound investment growth into the ultra-long term – for example, across generations – can transform entire family legacies. Wealth that compounds uninterrupted can create an exponentially different outcome to that which faces even occasional disruptions.

INVESTING SIMPLICITY: THE 20% THAT CAN DELIVER 80% OF RESULTS

If we can combine the discipline of maintaining contributions with the patience to let time do its work, we don't just transform the financial outcome but our relationship with money.

The power of compounding is a powerful ally. Pound-cost averaging allows us to harness the process, as it is consistent and automatic.

Average annualised market returns take account of a full market cycle – peaks as well as troughs.

> If you have a decades-long horizon as well as the risk appetite and sangfroid to sit tight during ups and downs, you can afford to stay fully invested in stocks .... Buffett has argued that the average investor only needs a straight-forward 90/10 portfolio – 90% in an equity tracker, and the rest in short-term bonds.[5]

Combining pound-cost averaging and a target investment allocation lays the foundation for a Pareto-efficient investment strategy that is simple to implement.

Consider the core elements of Pareto-efficient investing:

1 Choose a global index fund as your portfolio core (to capture systematic worldwide market returns) and any additional funds or bonds.
2 Set up automatic monthly contributions (to remove subjective timing decisions).
3 Focus on long-term goals, not short-term market volatility (to avoid emotional reactions).
4 Control costs and minimise complexity (to make the most of net returns).
5 Stay consistently invested (to harness the power of compound growth).

Moving beyond these simple building blocks requires significantly more effort, time, and expertise. Passive strategies are low-cost not just in financial terms but arguably even more so in emotional terms, as well as being less stress and less of a time commitment.

Focusing on the above will likely deliver most of the available market returns but with minimal complexity. In terms of your journey to financial independence, why put yourself in the position that you have to beat the market? In terms of aligning strategies with financial goals and time horizons, a more logical approach might be to take "just" enough risk to achieve your goals.

The beauty of such a Pareto-efficient investment strategy lies not in the sophistication but the elegant simplicity and proven effectiveness over time.

INTRODUCING EXCHANGE TRADED FUNDS

A great way, then, to start any portfolio is simply to buy the entire market. You can do this through purchasing an index tracker that tracks a broad index. The easiest way is to choose an Exchange Traded Fund (ETF) that tracks your chosen index.

Globally speaking, investors usually look at one of three size-weighted indices (where larger companies make up more of the index) created by two providers: FTSE and MSCI.

MSCI split their offering into MSCI World and MSCI All-Country World (the difference being that MSCI World focuses on the developed world, and MSCI All-Country World includes emerging economies – to the tune of about 10% of the index – in addition to the developed countries).

FTSE All World is like MSCI All-Country World in that it holds emerging markets to a similar proportion, but it goes further down the market capitalisation scale than MSCI World (the index being composed of the top 4,200 listed companies versus top 2,500 for MSCI). The composition of each index is therefore weighted slightly differently.

Generally, having chosen which index to track, when selecting which specific ETF to go with, the larger an ETF the better. A large fund allows for better liquidity and provides a larger base across which to apportion running costs.

MOVING BEYOND GLOBAL ETFS

For an investor looking to spice up their portfolio beyond this, in the hope of higher returns, it can be relatively easy to bring in satellite funds to complement the global ETF core, while maintaining a simple autopilot-based system each month. (Because of the weighted nature of a broad global index, an investor seeking emerging market or smaller company exposure, for example, may find their needs underserved by their main global ETF) – and could add an allocation to an emerging market fund, or active "smaller companies" fund alongside.

Similarly, it is very easy to use ETFs to take very active decisions. Nowadays, there seems to be an ETF for everything. An investor, concerned about the weighting of US tech stocks in a standard global ETF, could buy an ETF that tracks the world ex-USA and select an equal-weighted S&P 500 ETF to complement this, for instance. (The equal-weighted ETF contains all the S&P 500 companies but in equal proportion rather than market capitalisation, meaning that you own more of the smaller companies and less of the larger companies.)

THE 80% OF EFFORT THAT ADDS 20% TO RESULTS

The point is that investors can very quickly and easily produce a portfolio that is weighted very differently than a market "neutral" broad passive tracker. While there can be sound reasons for doing so, the overall point of investing is to arrive at an allocation that serves your needs, has the right amount of risk to deliver your goals, and that you can maintain to harness all the benefits of a Pareto-efficient investing strategy for the long term.

For many, there is simply no need to go beyond a simple global ETF to achieve this. For those venturing further, some of the traps of taking an active view have been covered in previous chapters. It is important to remain cognisant of these. (Also, for those that do, benchmarking performance against index funds is a good idea).

From a Pareto efficiency point of view, there is one more point to add to the list: *even if* such strategies ultimately prove successful, they might simply bring an element of fine-tuning to portfolio performance – one that adds far less in terms of marginal returns than the effort involved to obtain them. In other words, getting the extra 20% benefit can easily take up 80% of the overall effort.

CONCLUSION

At the end of the day, successful strategies do not have to rely on a lot of experience or skill, can involve little hands-on management, but can still be used to great effect even by beginners. You do not need to be an experienced investor, or to possess prerequisite analytical skills to achieve good results. A passive investment strategy can be effectively implemented and is a ready plan that can do much given time.

NOTES

1 FAANG stocks are a collective name for the five prominent US technology companies. The acronym stems from the first letter of each of their names: Facebook (now Meta), Apple, Amazon, Netflix, and Google (now Alphabet). This list has been expanded with the inclusion of Nvidia and Tesla into the so-called Magnificent Seven.
2 Norrington, James "Lessons from the World's Greatest Investors" (*Investors Chronicle*, 26 July–1 August 2024), page 24.
3 Kay, John *The Long and the Short of It* (Profile Books, 2016), page 241.
4 Kay, John *The Long and the Short of It* (Profile Books, 2016), pages 241–242.
5 Cipriani, Val "How to Truly Diversify Your Portfolio" (*Investors Chronicle*, 9–15 January 2026), page 21.

REFERENCES

Cipriani, Val "How to Truly Diversify Your Portfolio" (*Investors Chronicle*, 9–15 January 2026).

Kay, John *The Long and the Short of It* (Profile Books, 2016).

Norrington, James "Lessons from the World's Greatest Investors" (*Investors Chronicle*, 26 July–1 August 2024), pages 22–25.

21

A ROADMAP TO FREEDOM

Many people worry about whether they're saving enough; however, some are over-saving (which means denying themselves the opportunity to live their best life today), and others simply have no idea how to even get started.

Some people are already regular savers. Others may argue that they will save when they have something to save. Yet at the same time they will simply raise their expenditure, for example if they get a pay rise, and find themselves in an essentially unchanged position but with higher expectations.

As Robert Kiyosaki notes: "[A] person can be highly educated, professionally successful, and financially illiterate. … They're now trapped in the Rat Race."[1] Others can have a lot of the right knowledge but aren't sure how to structure a plan.

THE GAP ANALYSIS APPROACH

A starting point for many projects is to consider, first, where you would like to get to. In other words, what does the future look like to you? This vision of a desired future ("to be") state is valuable, because it allows you to critically assess and consider what you have today and how the two compare.

In my years working as a consultant, we used the contrast between the "as-is" situation and the "to-be" desired outcome to conduct a so-called gap analysis. In plain English, this means assessing the differences in "what is" to "what we would like it to be" and working out a plan on how to close the gap. If you know what you want to build, you can start to construct a plan to achieve it!

DOI: 10.4324/9781003792444-21

From a financial independence perspective, the "to-be" state is what you would like to achieve and when would you like to achieve it: do you want to own your own home? Where do you want to get to in terms of portfolio size? Do you want to change careers, go part-time, or stop work altogether? How soon?

These are just some of the variables.

PERFECT IS THE ENEMY OF GOOD

Consider this: your plan does not need to be perfect. You'll gain more of an understanding of what goals you are saving towards, how to get there, and investing in general once you have started. Many of these variables may even change, and that is OK. But by doing nothing and deferring the question for your future self to deal with at some unknown point in time carries absolutely no benefit – that much is certain. Plenty of people work hard in their careers but "stick their head in the sand" when it comes to financially planning for a life after work, hoping it will turn out OK. Doesn't it make more sense to have a plan with assumptions and variables you can tweak instead?

A lot of people will no doubt be looking at something much more optimal than this. After all, we lead complicated lives. How can you reduce this to simple rules? If you don't have access to a financial advisor, you have to rely on yourself. But why do you need a highly detailed, customised, bespoke plan on day one when much will no doubt change before you're ever anywhere near drawing an income from your assets?

Understanding some rules of thumb and some general guiderails to keep you on track is as sound a starting point as any. At some point in the future, you can (and probably should) refine and stress-test your plan with a financial advisor. Many people don't turn to an advisor until later in life. If you've been aiming at a good enough "ballpark," you may find that you end up not having to tweak your plan that much at all.

THE POWER OF SMALL DECISIONS

A multitude of tiny decisions – whether about savings, investing, or spending – contributes incrementally to achieving financial independence. These can be as varied as your spending habits, how much you save, how that money is invested, your attitude to debt, your career and salary, any side hustles or passive income sources, as well as – and this is important – your lifestyle choices.

There are benefits in starting to plan even if it means starting "messily." When do you plan to make a start if not now? "Action always beats inaction ... you must take action before you can receive the financial rewards. Act now!"[2] How you choose to spend your money will have a knock-on impact. The future could be viewed as the sum of "the choices you make today, not tomorrow."[3]

A financial plan can be a valuable aid not just in setting a course, but during the journey itself. It will also let you know when you are close to arriving at your destination. Each element can be equally precious.

STAYING THE COURSE

A well-constructed investment plan provides crucial psychological ballast during turbulent times. It serves as a reminder that you've prepared for market volatility and are following a time-tested predetermined strategy with historical precedent. History is on your side.

Use your plan as an emotional anchor: your investment plan truly proves its worth during periods of market extremes. When euphoria or panic grips the markets, the disciplined investor resists the powerful urge to abandon strategy.

By adhering to your predetermined approach, you remove emotional decision-making precisely when your instincts – and the market herd – push you toward potentially irrational choices. If the next market decline is like all the others, you will be "richly compensated" for staying invested.

This emotional discipline applies equally when greed, not fear, dominates. During bull markets, the temptation to increase exposure often means buying late in a cycle's uptrend. While markets do rise over the long term, deviating from your strategy rarely serves your interests.

Maintain your course, rebalancing when appropriate, but don't stray from it without solid compelling justification to do so. Discipline keeps you aligned with long-term financial objectives, preventing the classic mistakes of increasing risk exposure after sustained rallies or liquidating positions following prolonged declines.

A SIMPLE FINANCIAL PLAN

A financial plan can look surprisingly simple at its core:

1 Identify your baseline expenditure and discretionary spending (adjust as necessary).
2 Use the result to determine your financial independence number.
3 Think what work–life optimisation looks like for you and set your savings rate and timeline appropriately.
4 Consider your risk profile and set your target asset allocation.
5 Set up direct debits to automate your investments, tax-efficiently, to remove the biggest threat to your portfolio (your tinkering).
6 Keep going regardless of market noise to capture the long-term general upward trend in stock market prices.

Keep in mind how adopting a corporate approach can help achieve this:

1 Think strategically and be intentional with your money (such as corporate Treasuries do when assigning a purpose to each pound) and keep a budget accordingly.
2 Consider the "to-be" state that you want to achieve and construct a (business) plan to get there.
3 Adopt a risk management approach that prohibits outright speculation while setting target minimum (and maximum) asset allocation limits in order to manage inflation and portfolio longevity risk.

CASH FLOW MODELLING

"For many people … the moment it all becomes real is when they see their future in a cash flow forecast … in its simplest form, this can be done in a few columns and rows in a spreadsheet."[4] The formulas from this book, especially when used in combination, allow you to model a wide array of scenarios and construct a DIY plan in Excel – or to use in ad hoc analysis to answer specific questions. Such plans and forecasts can be as individual as you are and there is certainly not one right way of doing this.

> Some investors believe that for simplicity ... forecast models should only focus on real returns (that is, asset returns less inflation) ... while this approach is likely to result in lower projected wealth, it has the advantage of pricing your future income in today's money, which is usually better rooted in your understanding of spending.
>
> ...
>
> But ... there are [also] several very good (and free) DIY modelling tools available online ... all either provide tables or nifty graphic depictions of projected surpluses or deficits, as well as the timing and drawdown of various income sources in retirement.[5]

Your cash flow forecast should provide clarity, highlight potential shortfalls (as a cash flow forecast does for Treasury in the corporate sphere) and above all empower you by providing confidence in your financial decisions, to ensure work–life optimisation at every stage of life.

If you are still in doubt about putting a plan together yourself, it can't hurt to speak to a financial planner or coach.[6] It is important also to remember that your plan should remain a flexible tool; far from being set in stone, it should be revisited when anything changes materially, or at least periodically to check whether you remain on track or need to make any adjustments – to ensure your plan continues to remain aligned with your goals and circumstances.

THE PSYCHOLOGICAL CHALLENGE OF EARLY RETIREMENT

Finally, knowing where you are heading can be an invaluable aid in determining when you have arrived!

Financial security comes not just from the size of a portfolio but also from understanding how investments work and, in particular, how you can generate income from your portfolio — whether that is passive income such as via dividends, selling down investments in line with Bengen's 4% rule, or a more sophisticated plan drawn up with the help of a financial planner tailored to your unique circumstances.

At the point when an individual first becomes financially independent it might very well feel extremely uncomfortable to retire and lose the security of a salary coming in – even if that is what you were planning for. Granted, a pension can feel much like a salary, albeit a low one. However, with early retirement the state pension age might be years off, and your investment portfolio will need to take the strain until you receive even that. Kiyosaki, in his book *Rich Dad's Cash Flow Quadrant*, laments: "I have met many people who have millions in their retirement accounts and still feel insecure. Why? Because its money generated from their job or business. They often … know little or nothing about the subject of investments."[7] If you don't feel like you have enough, is there an amount of money that will actually make you content, and how do you go about determining what that is?

Against such a background, staying in work for "one more year" can exert a powerful pull. There might be sound reasons for doing so, such as if a stock market crash coincides with your planned retirement date. However, frequently it can be a case of the better you are at saving, the harder you might find it to retire and start drawing down. You have spent a career, perhaps, saving each month. When you end up drawing on your portfolio, you certainly wouldn't be the first to continue to save. But does your portfolio (still) really need you? There comes a point when what you are able to contribute has a diminishing impact. You worked hard to be in that position. If your pot can pay you your 4%, it is OK to spend that 4%. The scarcity mindset can be useful at certain points in your life – this might not be one of them.

Healthy life expectancy is below the state retirement age. It's important to consider that by the time you reach standard retirement age, on average, you may not have full health to begin enjoying it already at the point of retirement. This is a strong argument in favour of trying to bring retirement forward, not delay it unnecessarily.

Of course, delaying drawing down on the portfolio you've spent your working life building for another 12 months can mean another 12 months of growth, and at that time your portfolio will be considerable in size. An additional year's worth of potential growth is likely to be significant. (Not to mention the fact that you are also delaying drawing on it.) The two forces can work powerfully in combination. Yet what you put into the portfolio last may never be tapped other than by your heirs. That's fine if that's your intention, but be aware that the time spent working to increase the size of your estate could have been spent doing the activities you planned to do in your retirement, and it could be one less year of having full health in your retirement.

The power of an additional year can be something of a comfort blanket (or delaying tactic) in taking the step towards what you've worked your whole career to achieve – not just to be financially independent but to use it to buy the time to fully enjoy the fruits of your labour.

NOTES

1 Kiyosaki, Robert T. *Rich Dad, Poor Dad* (Plata Publishing, 2011), pages 72, 74.
2 Kiyosaki, Robert T. *Rich Dad, Poor Dad* (Plata Publishing, 2011), page 233.
3 Kiyosaki, Robert T. *Rich Dad, Poor Dad* (Plata Publishing, 2011), page 243.
4 Newman, Alex "How to Save Enough for Retirement" (*Investors Chronicle*, 13–19 October 2023), page 25. The ones mentioned specifically in the article are My NetWealth, Guiide, and the *Investors Chronicle*'s own pension calculator.
5 Newman, Alex "How to Save Enough for Retirement" (*Investors Chronicle*, 13–19 October 2023), pages 25, 26.
6 Newman, Alex "How to Save Enough for Retirement" (*Investors Chronicle*, 13–19 October 2023), page 26.
7 Kiyosaki, Robert T. *Rich Dad's Cash Flow Quadrant. Guide to Financial Freedom* (Plata Publishing, 2011), page 98.

REFERENCES

Kiyosaki, Robert T. *Rich Dad, Poor Dad* (Plata Publishing, 2011).

Kiyosaki, Robert T. *Rich Dad's Cash Flow Quadrant. Guide to Financial Freedom* (Plata Publishing, 2011).

Newman, Alex "How to Save Enough for Retirement" (*Investors Chronicle*, 13–19 October 2023).

22

THE WHOLE PICTURE

HEALTH, FINANCES, AND PURPOSE

Financial independence doesn't really have to be about retirement at all. It is a much broader question about the lifestyle that you would like to lead and then how you can achieve it on your terms.

Financial independence does not need to equate to giving up work. It can certainly get very nuanced. You can have a free life while remaining productive. You might want just enough financial independence to be able to switch to a lower-paying career in an area that you have real passion for, or where you feel you are making a difference.

You could semi-retire, switch to working part-time, or switch careers altogether. All of these scenarios could mean you still have some income coming in and will need your portfolio to do less than if you are retiring altogether.

Money, by itself, will never make you free. You probably need far less of it than you think, in financial terms, to be much freer than a lot of objectively wealthy people are. You certainly don't need to wait for the journey to complete before you can start enjoying freedom and to be able to start living the way you want to, once you are on the right track.

THE FIRE MOVEMENT: PROMISE AND PITFALLS

The FIRE (Financial Independence, Retire Early) movement builds on what in many ways is a very traditional view, which is "save, save, save." But another way of looking at this approach is "defer, defer, defer." The premise behind this can translate to having to wait until a magical point in the future when you get to

DOI: 10.4324/9781003792444-22

retire and finally start enjoying the fruits of your life's work. Many people in the FIRE movement will spend years living a life of denial (not just frugally but in some cases "ultra-frugally"), all with the aim of that "one day" to come.[1] Aside from the over-indexing of making sacrifices today, if the goal is accumulation, will they feel guilty about assigning a role to money other than its accumulation? They are basically riding two waves: trying to accumulate more faster; and asking their portfolio to do more than it needs to for average people. (Most people wouldn't aim for their portfolio to fund as much for so long.)

If you are planning to actually FIRE, it's probably not a bad idea to understand what your motivations behind never wanting to work again are. Are there actually any factors at play such as simply hating your current job? Is your career making you feel unfulfilled or do you think you have reached a dead-end? There is plenty that you can do that is far less drastic than retiring years early.

THE POWER OF INTENTIONAL MONEY MANAGEMENT

A huge advantage of planning your finances is that you can be intentional with your money and optimise work–life. You have the tools to ask: what impact does spending more today have on my future goals?

To keep focused, you *can* compound out the cost of major purchases in terms of how much that will cost your future pot (and there may be an advantage to doing so if you struggle with keeping to your budget). However, the flip side is also true. You may not need to be saving as much as you currently are. If you can quantify the track your finances need to be on, you have a tool to know if you could be spending more today guilt-free. That is powerful! Most people probably have no idea how this trade-off works in their own lives other than a vague sense that they *probably* should be saving more. Hopefully you now have useful tools to determine the right level for you and your long-term goals.

A scarcity mindset can lead to unnecessary frugality. FIRE provides a useful way of thinking about money, even if its application can be extreme. It's an antidote, nonetheless, to much of the criticism levelled at consumerist society and highlights the importance of saving as well as giving guiderails as to how much. This way of thinking gives you the ability to take control of your own financial destiny, quantify your savings goal, and understand how you can draw from your investments.

Beyond this, I'd encourage you to think about a balanced approach. Obsessing over a number is not a great way to live life. While it's great to be able to quantify how much is enough, getting there will take time.

THE ECONOMICS OF ENOUGH

"The Keynes generation of economists assumed that, as people became more efficient at satisfying wants, they would – and should as rational agents – work less and enjoy life more."[2]

In other words, if work is a means to obtain the things that we want to have, then as we accumulate wealth and the trade-off between money and time moves more in our favour, we could work less to satisfy the same wants; and we would rationally do so.

Skidelsky and Skidelsky found in practice the instability of human wants in (capitalist) societies fosters an "ethic of acquisitiveness" which "dooms" us to "continuous, objectless, wealth creation."[3] This economic insatiability, they hypothesised, is "rooted in human nature – in the disposition to compare our fortune with that of our fellows and find it wanting."[4]

One of the hardest skills in personal finance might be to get the goal posts to stop moving.[5]

"ENOUGH" AND THE HEDONIC TREADMILL

Scott Galloway writes, "[I]f money is the goal, you will never have enough."[6] In his book, he quotes a 1970s study by psychologists Donald Campbell and Philip Brickman on happiness (that involved lottery winners) and found that changes in life circumstances had "little measurable impact on happiness as we adjust to our new reality."[7] Campbell and Brickman "coined the term 'hedonistic treadmill' to describe what they were seeing in the data: no matter how much apparent progress we make toward our goal, we remain in the same place, spinning the treadmill faster."

The goal should not be to die with the most amount of money but to "buy the life you want!" John Bogle, founder of Vanguard, once told a story:

> [A]t a party given by a billionaire ... Kurt Vonnegut informs his pal, Joseph Heller, that their host, a hedge fund manager, had made more money in a single day than Heller had earned from his wildly popular novel *Catch-22* over its whole history. Heller responds, "yes, but I have something that he will never have ... enough."[8]

Real freedom can come from finding your purpose. If you then find a way for someone to pay you to do that every day, great. To build a financial pot to sustain you for a life after work in the traditional sense can take a long time. That can seem like an eternity if what you're doing every day for a living isn't something you enjoy doing. Money as the main motivation for career choice may not be the best reason for what is, after all, your life's work.

Any money you have left over represents experiences you could have had, things you could have bought. It's also time you could have spent with family or friends when you were working overtime or doing an extra shift.

Living an aligned life means evaluating that trade-off on the balance of probabilities and knowing how to set reasonable assumptions for them. My sincere hope is that it will be a life that's less stressful in terms of worrying about your finances. That better life can start today: less pre-retirement and post-retirement (less accumulation and drawdown phases of life) and living more aligned. You might find you are accumulating a very different type of pot – a pot of memories, of photos, of great stories of a life well lived, even while securing your future.

Once you've reached "your number," you may never need to work again – but what will you do all day? What is it that you're in a rush to get to, and what will you do with it once you get there? What will get you up in the morning are questions to consider well ahead of time.

Keynes wrote about the "psychological need to work" and "the old Adam" with us that we had to satisfy. "Work gives meaning to our lives; at any rate it saves us from the tedium of endless sloth."[9] Meanwhile, Skidelsky and Skidelsky defined leisure "not [as] a state of passive relaxation. It is a form of activity – activity undertaken for its own sake, and not for the sake of some external end."[10]

THE RISK OF OVER-SAVING

We started out by considering what it means to be financially independent and looked at a framework to get there. For many, that might initially mean having to get better at budgeting, and more intentionally allocating money, between necessities, discretionary spending, and saving. But this needn't mean making the saving of money a sport, or your money management may become advanced in certain areas but entirely lacking in the important component of how to spend that money! Our future self will thank us one day for taking care of the future as best we can, but it's important not to sacrifice today unnecessarily at the same time. If you really want to do something, why put it off? It's precisely this type of spending that gives you very memorable experiences and makes life worth living!

Financial independence is really only worth anything if we consider what opportunities that opens for us and so becomes inseparable from one of the really big questions in life: "What do I want to do with my life?" Financial Independence can mean not working, but then what? Who do you want to be?

We can't know the future. We can have a guess based on averages and probabilities. You could certainly add some nuance into this based on family history, but there are so many stories out there about people saying "I will do this and that when I retire" but then ending up not having a lot of time after all. This isn't a matter of being morbid, only realistic. It's also good to have dreams, but we need to be realistic enough to realise: "This is the moment!"

"You never know what will happen tomorrow: you are no more than a mist that is here for a little while and then disappears … yet you do not know what tomorrow will bring." There is a lot of wisdom in this Bible passage. The very next passage gives us further food for thought: "What you ought to say is: 'If it is the Lord's will, we shall still be alive to do this or that.'"[11]

FINDING YOUR BALANCE

Balance means developing a healthy relationship with money, and true mastery over our finances means thinking holistically. Money, in its essence, is a tool – neither good nor bad in and of itself. An important part of balance is first understanding and living within our means. Our savings rate can be used to measure how quickly we can achieve freedom. As mentioned, in some ways it is the most important element in reaching financial independence.

However, it's important to remember that while saving and investing are crucial and indispensable elements to achieving financial independence, they are only part of the equation. We must also remember to enjoy and spend our money. Life is to be lived and savoured. Our financial resources should enhance our experiences, bring joy, and create lasting memories that enrich our lives.

Respect your money, then, by living within your means, save and invest to secure your future, but beyond that spend joyfully to enhance your present. Good luck and best wishes on realising your purpose with balance – optimised to living the life that you want to live.

NOTES

1 FIRE has grown more nuanced than in its earlier days. There's now "Lean FIRE" and "Fat FIRE," for example. Lean FIRE followers typically reject materialism and live very frugal, low-cost lives to retire ultra-early. This is possible because their low-cost lifestyle enables very high savings rates. Fat FIRE conversely is about creating a luxury lifestyle but perhaps for many (again due to the savings rate required to achieve this) may simply be a doubling down on the deferral mindset until they reach their goal.

2 Skidelsky, Robert and Skidelsky, Edward *How Much Is Enough? Money and the Good Life* (Penguin, 2013), page 180.

3 Skidelsky, Robert and Skidelsky, Edward *How Much Is Enough? Money and the Good Life* (Penguin, 2013), page 180.

4 Skidelsky, Robert and Skidelsky, Edward *How Much Is Enough? Money and the Good Life* (Penguin, 2013), page 3.

5 Housel, Morgan *The Psychology of Money* (Harriman House, 2020), page 41.

6 Galloway, Scott *The Algebra of Wealth: A Simple Formula for Success* (Penguin, 2024), page 30.

7 Galloway, Scott *The Algebra of Wealth: A Simple Formula for Success* (Penguin, 2024), page 30.

8 Housel, Morgan *The Psychology of Money* (Harriman House, 2020), page 37.

9 Skidelsky, Robert and Skidelsky, Edward *How Much Is Enough? Money and the Good Life* (Penguin, 2013), page xiii.
10 Skidelsky, Robert and Skidelsky, Edward *How Much Is Enough? Money and the Good Life* (Penguin, 2013), page xiv.
11 James 4:14–15, *The Jerusalem Bible* (Darton, Longman & Todd, 1966).

REFERENCES

Galloway, Scott *The Algebra of Wealth: A Simple Formula for Success* (Penguin, 2024).
Housel, Morgan *The Psychology of Money* (Harriman House, 2020).
The Jerusalem Bible (Darton, Longman & Todd, 1966).
Skidelsky, Robert and Skidelsky, Edward *How Much Is Enough? Money and the Good Life* (Penguin, 2013).

23

AFTERWORD

The book you are holding is the culmination of a writing process that spanned nearly two years. During that time, it evolved significantly, becoming quite different from the book I initially set out to write. Its origins, however, stretch back much further – to long before I committed to writing it.

Years ago, I began drafting some guidelines about investing and financial management for my children, distilling the basics into easy-to-follow rules. Both are intelligent but, for reasons I can't fully understand, have little interest in finance beyond a vague awareness that they should know more. They are interested in short bursts, so having a basic list they could follow might one day serve them well.

Initially, the rules focused on budgeting – how to manage and accumulate capital to invest. Later, I added a "set-and-forget" investment approach, designed to be simple to follow without needing deep knowledge of the rationale. My hope was that this approach would work over the long term, regardless of what might be happening in the markets at the point of investment and would get them most of the way toward securing their financial futures.

As I've learned, books can take on a life of their own. Some ideas warranted deeper exploration than I had anticipated, while others required less attention or had, I felt, been well covered before. For example, the typical book on FIRE (Financial Independence, Retire Early) often includes piles of money-saving tips.

As the writing process unfolded, publishing proposals, reviews, and feedback from kind friends, colleagues, and associates helped to refine my thinking and steer the content in new directions. I

DOI: 10.4324/9781003792444-23

was surprised to find that many finance professionals, while deep experts in their day jobs, take a very different approach with regard their own finances. Financial planners were intrigued by my work experience and how it relates to the valuable job they do. Both added a further layer.

These contributions were invaluable, and I believe the book is far better as a result.

THANK-YOU LIST

I owe a debt of gratitude to more people than I can name. Over the years, countless conversations, analyses, projects, and career experiences have shaped the ideas that ended up in this book. Colleagues and friends reading these pages may recognise themselves, as well as the experiences or discussions – some from long ago – that stayed with me and influenced my thinking. I hope this book serves as its own form of thanks to all of you.

I am deeply grateful to everyone who contributed to this project. Writing this book has given me the opportunity to reflect on the various stations of my career, and I realise it is the unique blend of those experiences that made this book possible in the form you are holding in your hands.

A special thanks goes to the team at Taylor & Francis (Rebecca Marsh – Publisher, Business, Management, Economics; Grace Collier – Editorial Assistant; Jennifer Hicks – Production Editor; Gareth Vaughan – Copy Editor; Zoe Everitt-Spence – Squad Manager, Business, Economics and Law), who saw the potential in this project from the very beginning and supported me throughout the writing process. Your guidance and encouragement have been invaluable.

Thanks go specifically to László Bencsics Sr, Mária Bencsics, Gábor Bencsics, Miklós Bencsics, Anna Bencsics, Ági Szaniszló, Dóra Grausz, Bence Tóth, Richard Garry, Katharine Good, Gareth Wright, Andrew Cox, Nataliya Todorova, Craig Stevens, Sophia Gambardella, and the rest of Informa Group Treasury, Mahesh Ramaswamy, Edit Nagy, Mária Szabó, Paul Nemes, Dániel Varga, Thomas Knudsen, Eszter Csanádi, Jenny Ross,

Tünde Jáger, Dr Nóra Botos, Jesper Jonsson, Csanádi Lombardi, and all people who encouraged me.

Thank you all. I hope this book inspires you to take control of your financial future and live a life aligned with your values and goals.

Somewhere over the skies of Europe, 13 February 2026

INDEX

For Product Safety Concerns and Information please contact our EU representative GPSR@taylorandfrancis.com Taylor & Francis Verlag GmbH, Kaufingerstraße 24, 80331 München, Germany

Batch number: 10823841

Printed by Printforce, the Netherlands